The Future of the Democratic Left
in Industrial Democracies

Issues in Policy History
General Editor: Donald T. Critchlow

THE FUTURE OF THE DEMOCRATIC LEFT

IN INDUSTRIAL DEMOCRACIES

Edited by

Erwin C. Hargrove

The Pennsylvania State University Press
University Park, Pennsylvania

This work was originally published as a special issue of Journal of Policy History (vol. 15, no. 1, 2003). This is its first separate paperback publication.

Library of Congress Cataloging-in-Publication Data

The future of the democratic left in industrial democracies / edited by Erwin C. Hargrove.
  p. cm.—(Issues in policy history; #10)
Originally published as a special issue of Journal of policy history (vol. 15, no. 1, 2003) T.p. verso
Includes bibliographical references.
ISBN 0-271-02356-2 (pbk.)
1. Political parties—European Union countries. 2. Political parties—United States. 3. Political parties—Poland. 4. Political parties—Russia (Federation) 5. Right and left (Political science) I. Hargrove, Erwin C. II. Series

Contents

Editor's Preface

This collection reveals, above all else, that Western democratic regimes have entered into a new epoch in the twenty-first century. The ideologies of socialism and communism, at least in any pure form, appear no longer persuasive to party leaders, policymakers, and most voters. The collapse of communism in the Soviet Union and Eastern Europe, and the failure of many state-run enterprises in Western Europe, ended the intellectual attraction that centralized planning once had on political and intellectual elites in the West.

Similarly, while free-market economic ideology continues to exert influence in some political and policy circles, particularly in the United States and to a lesser extent in Central and Eastern Europe, capitalism in the West has been transformed by the emergence of broad-based social security and welfare systems, subsidized agriculture, and fiscal and monetary policy by central governments.

Any modification or repudiation of socialist, communist, or laissez-faire capitalist ideologies by political parties in the twenty-first century has not decreased, as Erwin Hargrove concludes, partisan conflict. The rival of the right in the United States, England, Italy, France, and Denmark in the post-1970 decades forced leftist parties to rethink their political programs and to move to the right on many economic issues. Challenged by an insurgent right, many leftist parties were forced to rethink their programs and political strategy in the 1970s in the light of stagnant economic growth and social discord. The collapse of the Soviet Union and the end of the Cold War accelerated this reevaluation.

Some parties on the democratic left sought a "third way," which accepted a more important role for the free market while promoting the older tradition of social justice through more efficient public programs in the new multicultural and multiracial society. This "third way" political strategy was most clearly articulated by neoliberals in the United States and by "New Labour" in Britain.

In other countries, democratic left parties pursued different strategies by forming political coalitions with new political groups such as "the Greens" that gained strength with the collapse of communist parties and the left in many countries. The Greens attracted younger voters concerned about the environment, economic globalization, finance capitalism, Third World poverty, and American military strength. By forming alliances with the Greens, the German Social Democratic party became revitalized after decades of Christian Democratic rule.

While democratic left parties in the United States, Britain, and Western Europe developed various strategies to preserve and, if possible, increase their political strength, as the authors in this volume show, social forces set a generally similar context for many of the Western democracies. In all these countries, aging populations brought about by a decline in native births imparted a disproportionate political influence to elder voters. The financial costs of maintaining elderly populations without a larger base of younger, employed people present a challenge to parties on the left and the right in every nation. Furthermore, within each nation the elderly have numerical strength to exert power at the ballot box that inevitably influences future social policies. Yet it is by no means certain whether this demographic shift benefits the right or the left. The elderly tend to demand (and vote) for more social and medical services. Thus the elderly present a natural constituency for left democratic parties that favor social justice through greater government social expenditures necessary to maintain Social Security and health-care programs. Yet, because the elderly often hold disproportionate wealth, they tend to favor low-taxation policies and general conservative fiscal policies, as long as such policies do not affect them. Low-taxation policies are the mainstay of most parties on the right.

Immigration also presents social problems in most Western democracies. Large numbers of newly arrived legal and illegal immigrants have changed political dynamics in most of these countries. Newer immigrants have tended to demand more social services, special education programs, and job training. Furthermore, demands for cultural and racial toleration have been raised because many of these new immigrants are people of color coming from different cultural and religious backgrounds from people in the host countries. These demands have caused political and cultural backlashes in many of the Western democracies, including France, Germany, England, Denmark, Italy, and the United States. Again, immigration is an issue that can cut either way politically, forcing the political right in more nationalist directions and the left toward rhetoric and policies that mobilize immigrant groups but alienate native populations, especially within the working class.

Immigrants play an important role in shaping what has commonly become known as "blue-red" voting patterns. Blue areas on a political map represent large urban areas with dense concentrations

of population, while red areas represent smaller cities and rural areas
with lower population densities. Because new immigrants often settle
in large urban areas, they are included in the blue population. Political
scientists have found that blue (urban) areas vote for left democratic
parties, while red (rural and smaller cities) vote for right democratic
parties. A surprising similarity in voting patterns has developed in many
Western democracies, including the United States, Britain (with the
exception of Scotland and Wales), and France. The electorates in these
countries are divided politically and ideologically, but overall narrow
margins have determined electoral success. Given the narrow margins
necessary to win an election, this should propel parties on the left and
the right toward the center in order to win swing or undecided voters.
The problem for political candidates facing a divided electorate where
a close voting margin will determine the final outcome of the election
is to maintain their core support while reaching out to voters in the
center, who are usually less politically informed and therefore less ideological and less partisan. This environment should force parties on the
left and the right toward the center, but this has not been the case in
recent national elections in the United States or France, where clear
ideological lines were drawn between candidates. In any case, divisions
represented by blue and red appear certain to remain in place in the
foreseeable future, given that unprecedented or catastrophic events do
not lead to massive shifts in the electorate, either toward the left or the
right. If the status quo remains, political parties and their candidates
will continue to confront rigid structural problems that will tend to
constrict political and policy innovation.

The essays in this volume are primarily concerned with the ideological development and political future of democratic left parties
in the West. The authors have addressed the central question posed
by the editor of the volume, Erwin Hargrove. The essays do not pre-
dict the future of the democratic left in the West; that future is still
to be decided. They do provide information and insights free from
the partisan polemics that fog many discussions. And while readers
are free to draw their own conclusions as to the future (although
they might wish a companion volume on the future of the democratic right were available to provide for a fully balanced conclusion), this volume will reward specialists and students who like to
think about what the political future holds.

Donald T. Critchlow
General Series Editor

ERWIN C. HARGROVE

Introduction

The purpose of this issue is to explore the possible political futures of parties and movements of the "democratic left" in the United States, the United Kingdom, France, Germany, the European Union, Poland, and Russia. The task could not proceed without clear definition, or definitions, of the "democratic left" because of national variations. There is "liberalism" or "progressivism" in the United States of many hues, but with no "social democracy" or politically viable socialism to the left. Socialism, in the old sense, of ownership of the means of production, has died in Britain, and the present government of "New Labour" refers to itself as the "Third Way" between capitalism and socialism. But there is much controversy at home whether "social democracy" has been also jettisoned in favor of a kind of "neoliberalism" that has embraced markets and trimmed social security. The large, democratic parties of the left in France and Germany derive from traditions of "social democracy" that have challenged many capitalist values and institutions, whether from Marxist or non-Marxist perspectives, and sought to establish a state and society organized around principles of social justice. These parties may win national elections but are torn between old left politics and the need to form larger coalitions in order to win. One might ask, Why include Poland and Russia? The purpose was to ask if new democratic forms of "social democracy" could be discerned in the ashes of defunct communist systems that might bear some resemblance to the politics of Western Europe.

So we are dealing with a sliding scale of definitions, but this is permissible so long as we are clear what we talking about. For example, to say "liberal" to Europeans may connote Margaret Thatcher and other free-market politicians who are not at all "conservative" in the traditional European sense. But "conservatives" in the United States are indeed Thatcherites in many ways. Definitions thus push us toward questions about American "exceptionalism" in the sense that the center of political gravity is further to the right in the United States than in Europe. But one must also ask whether the "Third Way" as seen in Britain, and in the Clinton presidency, and in its inroads into "social democracy" on the Continent, is not the converging future for democratic politics of the left.

As the editor, I posed a number of questions to the authors, recognizing that each question might not apply to all, but I aimed to hit a central theme in the politics of the democratic left:

1. If the traditional social bases of left parties are now too limited for winning in majoritarian politics, what kind of coalitions and ideas, which reach beyond those bases and yet retain them, may be effective?
2. If the answer to the first question is that such umbrella coalitions are too torn to be workable, what is the alternative? What is gained and lost in moves toward the center or further to the left?
3. Are coalition politics sufficient for governance in terms of both policy and the long-term political health of a party, or must there be a central, guiding set of ideas around which coalitions are formed?
4. What are the inherent weaknesses of market-oriented parties against which parties of the democratic left might appeal and win?
5. To what extent do national histories and political cultures both provide resources and set constraints and limits upon what parties may creatively do with political appeals and policies?

In the conclusion to the essays, I address these questions again and explore what a comparative analysis suggests about the future of the politics of the democratic left.

Vanderbilt University

ALONZO L. HAMBY

Is There No Democratic Left in America? Reflections on the Transformation of an Ideology

Historians historicize. They attempt to understand the present and make educated guesses about the future by looking to the past. This attempt at prognosticating "the future of the democratic left" primarily in the United States begins with a broad-brush history of "the left" as equalitarian idea and political movement in the modern world, examines its development in the United States within a context of "American exceptionalism," discusses its transformation in the 1960s, and assays its struggles in the "present day" of the last three decades. A once-revolutionary impulse, it suggests, has surrendered to the necessity of incremental entitlement politics. As a result, it has subjected itself to the hazards of the pragmatic test, the awkwardness of interest-group politics, and the distinct possibility that even success in the quest for universal social provision would fail to alter existing patterns of inequality.

The concept of "the left" is a European import that always has existed uneasily in the United States. Originating in revolution and placing its primary emphasis on the establishment of an equalitarian society, from the beginning it demonstrated the way in which the rationalism of the eighteenth-century continental Enlightenment was at odds with deeply rooted aspects of human nature. From the beginning also, the left has had to fight not simply oppressive reaction but another liberating ideology, a primarily Anglo-American liberalism that promoted liberty—defined as individual autonomy, inherent individual rights, and opportunity. It has especially struggled for existence in that most liberal of societies, the United States.

That we discuss the left at all in an American context at the beginning of the twenty-first century may be a tribute to its capabilities of survival and adaptation—as well as a certain talent for infiltration and disguise. The left, to the extent one exists in America, has appropriated the vocabulary of liberalism, and when all is said and done abandoned much of its original content and tone while clinging to remnants of its social objectives. Its history and persistence also say much about the aspirations and priorities of a politically minded intelligentsia with slender connections to the experience or outlook of the masses in contemporary middle-class democracies.

European Origins: The Age of Reason and the French Revolution: Marx and Modern Socialism

At the beginning of the French Revolution, the radical equalitarians clustered together on the left side of the seating in the National Assembly. Seeking to destroy a rigid, oppressive class system, the left promised the French a new utopian society of liberty, equality, fraternity. It delivered dictatorship, the rule of a new class, and terror.

Marx and Marxism followed in short order.

Marxism was in many respects a child of the Enlightenment. Based on materialist assumptions, it asserted a theory of inexorable historical progression from one stage of economic development to another toward a final socialist equalitarianism. It posited as its revolutionary force a new urban working class, nudged along to be sure by a vanguard of radical intellectuals.

In the world of reason defined by materialist assumptions, only economically determined social class mattered—not race, ethnicity, nationality, religion, gender, or numerous other indicators by which people identified themselves.

The task of overthrowing social institutions wholesale might seem to require violence of the sort employed throughout much of Europe by revolutionary anarchists. Yet by the last third of the century, the working class was effectively enfranchised in the Continent's most industrially developed countries, thereby raising the possibility of democratic political action. Facing a fork in the road, Marxian socialism took it. Depending on the locale, it could be either clandestine and violent or open and gradualist.

Why Was There No Socialism Anywhere?

"Warum gibt es in dem Vereinigten Staaten keinen Sozialismus?" Werner
Sombart asked in1906, referring to the absence of a strong socialist
political movement in the United States. Had he been lamenting
the absence of a fully developed socialism, he could have chosen his
country at random. Serious socialist movements aplenty existed in
Europe, but nowhere in the developed world could one find "socialism" in the form of a regime that had taken power, expropriated the
means of production, redistributed wealth, largely abolished private
property, and established substantial equality of condition. American exceptionalism was simply the most extreme point on a scale of
rejection.

The democratic left in Germany, the Social Democratic party,
became the most common descriptor for a nonrevolutionary incrementalism that pursued step-by-step progress toward the ultimate
goals of pure socialism. Its most controversial—and most visionary—
theoretician, Eduard Bernstein, even rejected Marxian theories of
historical development, asserting (correctly) that, contrary to movement theology, the conditions of the working class were improving,
a capitalist collapse was unlikely, and that Social Democracy might
flourish as a reform movement without reference to the ultimate
socialist vision. The Social Democratic leadership rejected
Bernstein's theoretical "revisionism" but in many ways followed his
practical political formula. A century and a quarter later, Bernstein's
incremental pragmatism had become the paradigmatic expression of
the Western democratic left. In the two larger economic powers to
the West—Great Britain and the United States—a socialist movement was much slower to develop. In Britain, intellectuals formulated a "Fabian Socialism" that provided some inspiration for
Bernstein. The erection of a political party, however, was a slow process. The Socialist movement in the United States was much weaker.
It produced no major thinkers, had no significant trade-union base,
and at its pre–World War I peak won only six percent of the presidential vote.

Why was there no socialism anywhere before World War I? The
answers varied from country to country, but the following general
answers apply to numerous political cultures:

> 1. The working class was more bound by tradition than Marxist
>   thinkers understood. Organized religion, whether social

Catholicism on the Continent and in the United States, non-conformist Protestantism in Britain, or the social gospel in the United States, constituted a significant part of the culture of many workers and frequently deployed programs of political action in their behalf.

2. The urban worker of the late nineteenth and early twentieth centuries was in general better off than his country cousins, however hard his life might be, the bucolic scenery of the countryside notwithstanding.

3. Traditional European conservatism, with its corporate sense of society and concept of cross-class obligations, provided a theoretical basis for concessions to the working class, whether the conservative leaders were Otto von Bismarck or Benjamin Disraeli. Frequently, conservatives could compete effectively for a good-sized slice of the votes of the working class.

4. So in some cases could centrist parties, most notably the pre–World War I British Liberal party of Herbert Asquith and Lloyd George and the Catholic-based German Center party. The exigencies of politics and the philosophical basis of Western liberalism would lead liberal parties everywhere to envision the concept of inalienable natural rights as including material issues.

5. Neither American political party was "conservative" by classical European definitions, but the Republicans of William McKinley, Theodore Roosevelt, and William Howard Taft demonstrated substantial appeal to the working classes. The Democrats under Woodrow Wilson (perhaps analogous to Asquith) made a promising run at constructing an organized labor core constituency in the 1916 election.

6. Nowhere was the "working class" the monolith that Marxian thought supposed it to be, and in most cultures it was not very revolutionary. "Unskilled" pick-and-shovel laborers, "semi-skilled" journeymen who performed routine operations in factory settings or transported goods, and "skilled" tradesmen who did precision work in a variety of settings all had different views of the world and varying incomes. Conditions of work encouraged different temperaments. Racial and ethnic identities often overrode class identity.

7. Different societies had different degrees of class stratification. Britain was more open than Germany, the United States considerably more so than Britain. Workers were probably

somewhat more likely to be homeowners in Britain than in Germany, much more likely in the United States than in Britain. Social fluidity and working-class property ownership were inimical to socialism.

The United States had never been receptive to socialism in the usual sense of the term, but its pervasive liberalism was hospitable to both capitalism and its critics. The dislocations of industrialism generated plenty of the latter, most of them not socialists, but populist agrarians and labor unionists. Convinced that they were victims of big business and finance, these groups spoke to a quintessential American theme by demanding more equality. Both frequently employed rhetoric that suggested the United States was trending in the direction of class-ridden Europe. Both reserved many of their harshest condemnations for "capitalists" and capitalism. In general, however, their objectives were not revolutionary. Rather, they envisioned politics or industrial action as a means of self-advancement. They also helped precipitate a middle-class reform impulse ("progressivism") that sought to check the excesses of capitalism and provide in various ways for groups that had been left behind.

The closest approximation to a significant revolutionary response, the Socialist party of Eugene V. Debs, threatened to become the U.S. version of the German Social Democratic party. Debs, a native of Terre Haute, Indiana, and a product of Midwestern labor battles, could proclaim his identity as a native son, however much his often fiery speeches read as if they were the work of central European Marxists. Debs's charisma and the emergence of what looked to be a genuine challenge to capitalism led to apprehension at the time, but the Socialist party never amounted to much more than distant thunder from the left. With few exceptions, American trade unions took the pragmatic course of bargaining for more pay and fewer hours within the capitalist system rather than adopting the more problematic strategy of trying to overthrow it. Locally, the party managed to control a few small and medium-sized industrial cities, but mostly on the basis of good government, efficient administration, and control of public utilities rather than wider-ranging platforms. Election results revealed the limits of its national appeal. A five-time candidate for president, Debs achieved his greatest triumph in the 1912 election with six percent of the total vote; he never came close to carrying a single state or winning a single electoral vote. Socialist representation in Congress and state legislatures was likewise insignificant. Debsian socialism never won over more than a small fraction of the working class and its unions. Still, it easily could be mistaken in the early twentieth century for a growing force analogous to the Labour party on the other side of the Atlantic.

Interwar Years: Openings and Roadblocks

World War I seemed at first glance to have created new opportunities for socialism, democratic and otherwise. War itself, as Randolph Bourne observed, was the health of the state, enlarging its power, requiring mass mobilization and collective effort. It also enabled previously marginalized or disaffected groups to press claims for recognition and benefits. The war demonstrated conclusively that working classes affirmed their national identities as far more important than their class identities, but its aftermath also appeared to open doors to the left in one country after another. In Weimar Germany, the Social Democratic party was from the beginning the strongest political force. The British Labour party emerged in the 1918 election as the nation's second party. With Liberal support, it was able to form two short-lived governments (1924; 1929–31), but lacking a majority in the House of Commons, it could not implement a fully developed socialist platform.

Perhaps most fatefully, the war not only gave a boost to the democratic left, but it also produced a serious burden in the form of the Soviet Union. Under Lenin as well as Stalin, the Soviet Union quickly established itself as a socialist dystopia that confirmed the lessons of the French Revolution and became a loathsome example invoked by antisocialist forces in one democratic country after another. It also split the left everywhere, severing revolutionary factions from predominantly democratic gradualist movements and establishing separate Communist parties. The Soviets, asserting themselves as the only legitimate voice of socialism, established the Communist International, controlled the new parties, and became the most vehement enemies of the democratic left. In Germany, the relationship between the two parties, which combined would have been just a few percentage points short of an absolute majority, was one of bitter hostility. The same enmity developed in other countries. What might in a united party have been a debate over the pace of change had become a fundamental difference of principle. A multinational radical intelligentsia, desperate to find something of value in the "Soviet experiment," praised its national economic planning and made rather too much of the meager benefits it bestowed on previously neglected classes. In most of the Western world, majorities sensing the emergence of what would come to be called "totalitarianism" recoiled in horror.

One might expect the Great Depression, a cataclysmic crisis of capitalism, to have created new opportunities. Instead, almost everywhere, the Depression created an upsurge of national sentiment that was not compatible with the socialist vision, democratic or otherwise. The major democratic countries either embraced a squishy centrist reformism, as in the United States and Britain, established no clear direction, as in France (where Leon Blum's United Front cabinet lasted only a year), or lurched to the authoritarian right, as in Germany. In Europe, the model for the future seemed more likely to be the one already established by Antonio Salazar in Portugal and Benito Mussolini in Italy—fascism. A loose adaptation of medieval corporatist thought to modern industrial society, fascism accepted all economic classes as legitimate, subordinated individual aspirations to a common vision of national destiny, and posited a strong authoritarian state as the mechanism that would harmonize society. Its primary assumption, which seemed demonstrated in much of central and Mediterranean Europe, was that majorities everywhere feared class warfare and were, when pressed, willing to trade liberty for stability.

Among the large nations of Europe, Britain provided the clearest example of a successful democracy from which the democratic left was excluded. Its National coalition government was effectively a Conservative party regime in which Stanley Baldwin was chairman of the board and Neville Chamberlain the chief operating officer. It pursued policies of fiscal conservatism, high taxes, protective tariffs, industrial stabilization, and social provision (primarily the dole and subsidized council housing). In 1931 and 1935, it won the two greatest British electoral victories of the twentieth century. Its leaders depicted themselves as following a middle way between Communism and Fascism—carrying the "torch of freedom" in Europe, as Baldwin put it.[1] In truth, the government's policies worked at least as well as those advanced by their persistent critic John Maynard Keynes would have, achieving recovery by late 1935 without incurring Keynesian deficits.

There was, however, yet another interpretation of the middle way, one somewhere to the left of Keynes. The Scandinavian nations emerged from the Depression with democracies intact and regimes sometimes described as socialist. But the Scandinavian path was typified by highly developed welfare states supported by high taxation that substantially redistributed income. Regulation of major industries was extensive, government ownership relatively small. Independent cooperatives received government support. Such arrangements were perhaps more feasible in small, homogeneous countries, where it was but a slight exaggeration to say that everyone was related to everyone else, than in large, heterogeneous industrial democracies. But the move toward equality without revolutionary turmoil and with widespread acceptance won the attention of democratic leftists everywhere in the 1930s—not least those in the United States.

America Becomes More Exceptional, 1919–1939

If in Europe World War I seemed to create openings for a democratic left, it closed the door in the United States. The war may have strengthened European socialist parties, but it destroyed their American counterpart. American socialists, unlike their European comrades, opposed the war and suffered extensive persecution for it. The establishment of the Moscow-controlled U.S. Communist party split American socialism severely. Most important, the war left the United States with none of the socioeconomic hangover that afflicted the major European nations. After a sharp but brief economic downturn, the economy soared to unprecedented levels of prosperity in which labor shared more fully than ever before, thus giving the lie to standard socialist doctrine that capitalism progressively impoverished the working class.

In 1924, the Socialist party supported Robert La Follette Sr.'s insurgent Progressive candidacy in what amounted to a tacit admission that it had abandoned the objective of socialism as that word was generally understood. In 1928, its new leader, Norman Thomas, undertook the first of six presidential candidacies, embarking on a career of condescending acclaim from an establishment that respected his candor and never had the slightest fear of him. Thomas, however, was by no means inconsequential. He never outright rejected the ultimate goal of an equalitarian socialist reorganization of society, never renounced his vaguely Marxist frame of reference, and always clung to a dogmatic pacifism rooted in the belief that wars were the product of capitalism. But he also involved himself in incrementalism to a far greater degree than had Debs. Perhaps his proudest hour came during the 1930s, when, at real personal risk, he joined efforts to organize impoverished and oppressed Arkansas share-croppers. By such actions, he implicitly affirmed that the road to equality could be reasonably traversed one slow step at a time, that a socialist could be a liberal in a hurry as well as a revolutionary.

The Great Depression did no more for the American left than for its European counterpart. The U.S. democratic manifestation was livelier and more visible than ever, displaying formidable intellectual firepower in the persons of John Dewey and Reinhold Niebuhr, policy advocacy in such left-leaning economists as Paul H. Douglas, and political leadership across a range that included Fiorello La Guardia, Philip and Robert La Follette, Floyd B. Olson, Tom Amlie, and Maury Maverick. These and other individuals came together in the newly formed League for Independent Political Action, talked of forming an alliance with the Socialist party, and expected to establish a new political force that would displace the Democratic party with its halfway reform programs. Yet Franklin Roosevelt's New Deal, for all its inconsistencies and halfway measures, also had appeal. A British observer could find in it elements of both national coalition conservatism and Keynesian liberalism. Radicals scoffed at its early National Recovery Administration as "state capitalism" and derided its later neopopulist business bashing as retrograde. But Roosevelt provided relief for the jobless and federally funded welfare for the weak on an unprecedented scale. New Deal programs such as the Tennessee Valley Authority engaged in breathtaking socioeconomic planning. Moreover, Roosevelt remade the Democratic party, minimizing the importance of its former Southern-rural base and establishing a new Northern-urban-labor base not unlike those of social-democratic parties in Europe. Half-critical, half-supportive, unable to agree on a platform of opposition, the democratic left watched with fascination as FDR swept to victory in 1936. Those who had both political ambition and a sense of realism were inexorably drawn into his orbit.

The wave of the future had been demonstrated as early as 1934, when Upton Sinclair, the old socialist novelist and pursuer of noble lost causes, registered as a Democrat, entered the party's gubernatorial primary, capitalized on a latent wave of sentiment for change among its rank and file, and won. That fall, he campaigned for the statehouse on a platform of utopian socialism that he called EPIC (End Poverty in California). He lost, of course, but by a margin far narrower than would have been the case had he campaigned as a member of the Socialist party. Sinclair's large vote, despite a career in which he had embraced numerous fringe causes, demonstrated that the message of the left, if presented on the Democratic voting line, could attract mass support. If presented smoothly by a less vulnerable candidate than Sinclair, it could perhaps be a winner.

A few third forces emerged at state or local levels, but even they tended to be attracted to FDR and what he stood for. Perhaps the most significant example was the creation of the American Labor Party in New York by the socialist Amalgamated Clothing Workers Union. Its explicit purpose was to provide a vehicle that would allow committed leftists to cast a ballot for Roosevelt. By the end of the 1930s, realists understood that the future of the democratic left was as the Democratic left.

World War Again: America Becomes Less Exceptional

The experience of World War II set the stage for a resurgence of the left, democratic and otherwise, in much of Europe. Both were on the side of history in the struggle against fascism. In the East, the Red Army imposed Communist-leaning governments in one country after another; these soon became outright Communist regimes that ruthlessly suppressed all opposition. In both East and West, the left derived inspiration and moral influence from various national myths of resistance that stressed an ideology of democratic equality. Fascist tendencies survived only on the Iberian Peninsula. In France and Italy, Socialist and Communist parties regularly accounted for between forty and fifty percent of the vote in national elections, while controlling many cities and labor unions. However, they remained divided on critical issues of democratic values and allegiance to Moscow. Socialists participated in larger shifting coalitions, but "the left" never gained power in the sense of establishing a unified, stable government. In West Germany, politics settled into a contest between the Christian Democratic party, at its core a revival of the prewar Catholic Center party, and a revived Social Democratic party that shed much of its Marxist dogma for a more pragmatic platform of social provision for the masses. The Social Democrats would finally come to power under Willy Brandt in 1969.

Among the major nations, only in Britain did the left achieve an unambiguous popular mandate with the surprise victory of the

Labour party in 1945. Although Labour had opposed rearmament until very late in the game during the 1930s, the Conservative leadership of the prewar era took most of the blame for unpreparedness and appeasement. In Britain, moreover, the political left was not divided. During the war, Britain, under attack but never occupied, maintained a lively democratic politics in which sacrifice and collective effort bred a widespread sense of equalitarianism and democratic entitlement. Labour, a full partner in a coalition war government, managed much of the home-front activity. It also produced the Beveridge Plan, which laid out a postwar social policy that would feature a national health system, family allowances, comprehensive social insurance, and measures to achieve full employment. The Beveridge Plan became the most popular talking point of the British left and restored Labour to the fully competitive position it had briefly occupied after World War I.

The United States, viewed through the lenses of national elections and large political trends, could not have been more different. For all its success in waging war, the Roosevelt administration was constantly on the defensive at home. The regimentation necessary to prosecute the war manifested itself in the form of shortages, price controls, and rationing that were daily nuisances in the lives of ordinary consumers, businessmen, farmers, and workers. Geographically isolated from combat, Americans were freer to focus on constant irritations inflicted by a New Deal government that, rather than providing benefits of one sort or another, seemed to be denying them the fruits of prosperity. When the National Resources Planning Board, a small government agency staffed by New Deal policy intellectuals, published its own version of a Beveridge Plan for America, Congress terminated it. President Roosevelt's 1944 campaign calls for a revival of the New Deal rallied his core support but generated little enthusiasm from the wider electorate. He won reelection by his slimmest majority. Two years later, with Roosevelt dead and succeeded by Harry Truman, voters reacting against a multitude of annoyances returned Republican majorities to Congress.

Yet beneath the pattern of defeat, a new American left had emerged. Activist, democratic, and increasingly influential within the Democratic party, this force was no longer sharply distinguishable from the supporters of the New Deal. Its theme was not widespread government ownership or the ultimate abolition of private property—still the rhetorical goal of European socialist parties. Tempered by a realistic understanding of the possible on the American side of the Atlantic, it advocated widespread social benefits in the spirit of the Beveridge Plan. To this it tacked on Keynesian-inspired government fiscal manipulation of a capitalist, market-driven economy. Labour's 1945 victory gave American liberals exhilarating examples of implementation. The establishment of the National Health Service was a particularly stirring example of the promise of government welfarism. A proposed American version, first advocated by Truman in 1945, almost immediately became a standard plank in the national platform of the Democratic party. Truman's larger proposed "Fair Deal" program included large programs and investments in expanded social insurance, housing, education, family farming, and public electrical power.

The new mood of the American democratic left was most memorably captured by the thirty-two-year-old Harvard intellectual Arthur M. Schlesinger Jr. in his book *The Vital Center* (1949). Written in the wake of Henry Wallace's failed pro-Communist Progressive party insurgency of 1948, it rejected the idea of a linear ideological progression from the right to the left. Instead, Schlesinger posited fascism and communism as more alike than not and nearly indistinguishable in their hostility toward individual liberty and constitutional government. Heavily influenced by Reinhold Niebuhr's neo-Calvinist theology, he rejected revolutionary utopianism as beyond the capacity of human nature and destined to culminate in chaos or totalitarianism. The Soviet Union, he asserted, had to be rejected by democrats of the left. Such cautions were not meant as a plea for a timid centrism, however. Schlesinger approvingly cited Labour and other European movements of the non-Communist left, making it clear there and in other writings that he saw the valid path of American liberalism as a gradual march toward an outcome that might be best described as social democracy.

In the postwar era, British Labour was more than a distant example to many figures on the American left. American liberal Democrats and British Labourites increasingly identified with each other and at times participated in each other's campaigns.[3] Both movements quickly marginalized Communist and pro-Communists, accepted the reality of Soviet totalitarianism, and pursued equalitarian domestic agendas. Both found organizational bases in democratic trade-union movements. In the United States, much of the labor base was the Congress of Industrial Organizations (CIO), an amalgam of mostly unskilled and semiskilled workers that the New Deal had midwived in the 1930s. Its first president, Philip Murray, was a product of Catholic social movements; his successor, Walter Reuther, had learned democratic socialism from his father. It was not simply on whim that President Truman chose to begin his 1948 election campaign with a Labor Day rally in Detroit's Cadillac Square, or that his successors followed his example for the next twenty years. The Democratic party was no American Labour party, and its liberal element rarely had effective control of both houses of Congress. But at the level of presidential nominations and elections, the liberals were clearly its dominant faction, a party within a party loosely replicating the structure and outlook of their British counterparts.

In the end, of course, the Democratic presidential agenda was no match for the forces of traditionalism arrayed against it—the large majority of the Republican party, resolutely middle-class, predominantly old-stock, and business-oriented; and the minority Democrats in Congress, rural, Southern, tenaciously suspicious of big government, labor unions, and Northern ethnoreligious minorities. Most of all, it was overwhelmed by the unexpected and rapidly spreading prosperity of the postwar years. In contrast to the agonizing fifteen years of depression and war that had preceded the end of World War II, the period 1945–60 was one of rapid economic expansion, punctuated to be sure by brief recessions, but steadily raising the standard of living of most Americans. In particular, the success of labor unions at their baseline economic function of collective bargaining undermined their secondary mission of social reformism. Well-paid workers driving new automobiles to work from three-bedroom homes in middle-class suburbia were not shock troops of social change. Capable of picketing with some feeling in the event of a strike, they nonetheless wanted "more," not equality, not management responsibility, not nationalization.

Even many policy intellectuals believed that the "distributional problems" of society had been largely solved. The most influential of liberal economists, John Kenneth Galbraith, described himself in unguarded moments as a democratic socialist. Yet Galbraith asserted in *The Affluent Society* (1958) that the problem of poverty had been reduced to an "afterthought" in America, save for a few depressed areas.[4] Still an enthusiastic—indeed uncritical—advocate of government management of the economy, he now saw the main problem of America as one of too much frivolous private consumption. A starved public sector, he argued, needed more funding primarily to enhance the amenities of collective cultural life rather than to provide necessities to the needy.

By 1960, the Democratic left had largely absorbed American socialism.[5] It had developed an ambitious agenda, a substantial power base, and more political influence than ever, but power remained beyond its grasp. In fact, the prevailing political mood seemed to be turning against it. Eisenhower and the Republicans had accepted the established programs of the New and Fair Deals, whittling away only where they safely could and fighting new initiatives, such as more federal electrical power. Universal health insurance as a political issue shrunk to advocacy of federal medical care for the elderly, which itself was reduced to a minor means-tested program in the Kerr-Mills Act of 1960. Political winds were blowing the same way in most of the rest of the Western world. Conservatives had returned to power in Britain in 1951; they accepted the socialist welfare state much as Eisenhower accepted the social programs of the New Deal. In West Germany, the Christian Democrats achieved a fabled "economic miracle" and seemed destined to remain in power forever. Ambitious social reformism appeared stalemated. In fact, however, a tumultuous new era was just around the corner.

New Politics, New Lefts, New Dead Ends

In the dozen years from 1960 to 1972, the character and objectives of the American left changed profoundly in ways that created both large opportunities and large stresses, brought forth new constituencies but alienated old ones. A traditional left, politically based in organized labor and advocating an ever-expanding welfare state, gave way to a messier New Left that was a mélange of black activists, student protesters, cultural dissidents, and antiwar forces. Within these groups one could find cadres of revolutionaries who spouted recycled Marxist rhetoric (although even these frequently preferred to call themselves "Maoists"). But for most of those who participated in the upheavals of the time, the revolution was about other things—the empowerment of a race, the liberation of women, the legitimation of homosexuality, the construction (primarily among the young) of a new morality that in many respects amounted to an inversion of the old, an antimaterialism that reflected the boredom of affluence, a near-primal urge of the "young" (a category older in age than any generation of "young" before it) to throw off the dominance of parents and authority figures, and a rejection of the Vietnam War. The most famous of the anti-Vietnam slogans, "Make Love,

Not War," neatly expressed much of the ethos of the new movement. The old radicalism of class was seldom heard. Opposition to
Vietnam tended to be more widespread among the children of the
affluent rather than those of blue-collar workers or ethnoreligious
minorities, although the latter groups were much more likely to be
drafted into the armed forces. The "workers," who tended to be well-
paid cultural traditionalists, were downright hostile to antiwar forces
and counterculturalists. Their unions mostly took the same attitude
and tended to be despised by the newer radicals as establishment
institutions. To a startling extent, what had developed was a radicalism without a working-class base.

The most important contribution came from the civil rights
movement, which swelled to a mighty tide in the 1960s. The movement established a paradigm of protest, moral suasion, and political
power that quickly would be copied by other groups. In a liberal
society, claims of oppression and victimhood had a way of attracting sympathy and conferring political power. To one degree or another, and with varying degrees of merit, the formula would be
employed by other groups claiming mistreatment or discrimination—
feminists, gays, lesbians, American Indians, and the handicapped,
among others. The 1960s created a culture of protest, especially
alluring to younger people, that would hang on in one form or another long after the decade itself had become a matter of historical
curiosity.

The redefinition of the left and its causes might have excluded
class altogether if not for another surprising development of the
1960s—the rediscovery of poverty. A landmark book, *The Other
America* (1963) by Michael Harrington, a dedicated young Socialist, demonstrated persuasively that by reasonable income measure-
ments, one in every five Americans was poor—not perhaps clothed
in rags, seriously malnourished, or shelterless, but hardly privileged
in these respects and certainly apt to be poorly educated and lacking
adequate medical care. Harrington did not explore carefully numerous issues such as causes and duration of impoverishment. But he
did successfully show that American poverty was greater than generally believed and was widely distributed geographically. The rediscovery of poverty and the understanding that it was most prevalent
among those minorities who would soon be described as "people of
color" brought class oppression back into American politics, united
it with race, and gave the democratic left a cause that went beyond
the cultural trends of the white middle class.

All these seething trends came together in the middle years of the 1960s. The presidency of John F. Kennedy had pursued a mainstream liberal agenda of economic growth, coziness with organized labor, and assistance to depressed areas. Late in the game, it had been forced to propose a major civil rights bill by black protests in Birmingham, but in general its impulses, domestic and foreign, had been well within the parameters of a mainstream Cold War liberalism that juggled the demands of the varying constituencies within the old New Deal coalition.

Lyndon Johnson came to the presidency most likely expecting to continue in the same path, but with greater achievement. Given unexpected leeway in 1964 by the electorate's rejection of Barry Goldwater's challenge from the extreme right, he succeeded beyond his greatest expectations. Johnson's Great Society agenda appeared at first the fulfillment of objectives established by Roosevelt and the New Dealers, but it was so different in scale as to be different in kind. Yet Johnson's pursuit of war in Vietnam set off a leftist backlash. In the end, he himself would become the victim of a political revolution his programs had done much to touch off. There seemed much to applaud in the Great Society—two epochal civil rights acts, Medicare for the elderly, greatly expanded "medicaid" for the nonelderly needy, generous expansions of the traditional Social Security programs, a nondiscriminatory immigration act, major aid to education, large urban development and housing programs, and manifold antipoverty efforts. In what was surely a historic first, Johnson or someone on his staff arranged for Michael Harrington, still a registered socialist, to lecture the cabinet on poverty, thus ratifying in yet another way the practical assimilation of the once autonomous voice of the democratic left into the Democratic party. The Great Society represented the enactment of almost the entire agenda of a left-liberal intelligentsia concerned with great issues of social policy.

Just as revolutions often devour their leaders, they also generally have negative, unintended consequences. Rather than simply provide a satisfying response to legitimate black grievances, the civil rights acts seemed to generate an upsurge of riot-prone black militance. Whatever the statistical dent in the incidence of poverty, the array of programs to alleviate it seemed to encourage social dysfunction that included crime, the emergence of a steadily growing welfare class, and growing illegitimacy. Large-scale new entitlements such as Medicare, Medicaid, and expanded Social Security benefits generated little controversy in the beginning but were budgetary time bombs. To the consternation of Johnson and others in his administration, the Great Society was assailed not simply by conservatives who denounced large expenditures and a big expansion of the state, but equally by liberals who attacked it as a timid first step.

Even without the Vietnam War and the inflation that accompanied Johnson's uncritical embrace of guns and butter, the Great Society would have been bitterly contested. Too many of its components were poorly conceptualized. Some of its advocates, who saw its most important effect as income redistribution, never stated such a goal frankly. Historically, American liberalism had proclaimed the goal of equality of opportunity. The new liberalism of the Great Society, reflecting the influence of what once would have been an independent left, talked opportunity but in practice sought to establish an entitlement state in which inequalities would be minimal and government would provide for everyone. Majority support for what Gareth Davies has described as a move from "opportunity to entitlement" was nonexistent.[6] Equalitarian radicalism was once again running up against the limits of a pervasive liberal tradition.

Johnson and the Great Society also faced another problem. Two-party politics in America had always required the building of grand coalitions composed of interest groups that in the best of circumstances had scant common ground. Ideas and broad policies, if compellingly expressed by an imposing leader, could provide a sense of unity. But Johnson was steadily less imposing, and the ideas he had given free rein had little currency in American politics. By 1968, the Democratic party, especially as seen on television at its national convention, appeared to be composed of clusters of interest groups with little coherence and at times in open combat with one another. The war, overshadowing everything else, was the prime motivation in Johnson's decision to retire. One may question, however, whether he and the Democrats could have prevailed in an electoral debate that focused on his domestic program.

George McGovern's candidacy in 1972 underscored such doubts. McGovern won the nomination running as the candidate of left-liberals newly empowered by a revision of delegate selection rules that he had supervised. The new process pushed aside old bastions of traditional liberal support such as urban machines and much of organized labor. McGovern's platform, calling for a broad enlargement of the Great Society right down to minimal state income provision for every person in the country and advocating what could be fairly described as a pacifist foreign policy, was nothing if not frank about its hopes of a social and economic revolution. Prominent among his enthusiasts were representatives of the countercultural forces that had emerged in the sixties and added their various causes to the liberal agenda. It was particularly noteworthy that organized homosexuals made their first appearance as a factor in national politics at the convention that nominated him.

McGovern's candidacy proved that in optimal circumstances a cutting-edge left could control a Democratic presidential nomination. It also demonstrated that the Democrats were less coherent than ever; centrist elements of the party deserted in droves. In November, the electorate rejected McGovern as resoundingly as eight years earlier it had rejected Goldwater's rightist challenge to American political norms. The left, one might conclude, had seen its day in the Democratic party. Or had it?

What's Left? Reformulation and Repackaging from McGovern to Clinton and Gore

A reaction against McGovernism within the Democratic party was inevitable. What was surprising was the shape it took. By mid-1976, McGovern had been replaced on the ballot, not by a Northern, urban politician supported by Democratic machines and big labor, but by a one-term governor from a mid-sized Southern state. Jimmy Carter was to a great extent the beneficiary of a national longing for an attractive fresh face in American politics, but he was also the harbinger of an emerging trend in American politics. A Southern "moderate" who had won endorsement from black civil rights leaders, Carter packaged himself as a committed liberal who possessed administrative and budgetary skills not usually associated with that persuasion. Without questioning the social goals of liberalism, he displayed a skeptical attitude toward big spending and bureaucratic regulation. During his presidency, he would actually initiate airline deregulation. The first post–Great Society Democratic president, he represented a movement that had taken shape in reaction to it— "neoliberalism."

More an attitude than a solid body of doctrine, neoliberalism had two core assumptions. The first was a sense that the Democratic party had become little more than a disparate body of interest groups seeking favorable policy consideration and subsidies from Washington.

The second was a growing conviction that many programs connected with liberalism did not meet important pragmatic tests; business regulation, for example, often operated to the advantage of the regulated by foreclosing healthy competition or maintaining rates and prices at above-market levels. Lurking behind these assumptions was a growing revival of neoclassical economics, but also a quest for a public interest that could be invoked to transcend the claims of squabbling factions. In the end, however, neoliberals were less at odds with the fundamental assumptions of the Democratic left than confident they could achieve its objectives with greater efficiency.

The Carter presidency crashed and burned, not because of neoliberalism but mostly because of Carter's inability to put it into effect. Carter succeeded only in generating hostilities with the left wing of his own party. Inept in dealing with Congress, unable to control spending, managing the economy disastrously, he more often than not seemed a prisoner of the forces he had been elected to tame. Moreover, his foreign policy (an area in which no coherent neoliberal position would ever emerge) went very badly. What is intriguing is that Carter's failures, capped by Ronald Reagan's big victory in the presidential election of 1980, did little to derail the growth of neoliberalism.

To understand why, one must glance briefly at Western Europe. By the time Ronald Reagan took the oath of office as president in January 1981, Conservatives under the aggressive antistatist leadership of Margaret Thatcher had been in power for the better part of two years. She and her successor, John Major, would run Britain for nineteen years. In Germany, after the Social Democratic party dumped its moderate leader, Helmut Schmidt, the Christian Democrats won the 1982 elections under Helmut Kohl, who would dominate the nation's politics for a decade and a half. Socialists under President François Mitterrand hung on in France precariously, until they sustained losses in the 1986 legislative elections, which paved the way for a two-year premiership by Jacques Chirac. Mitterrand would win reelection as president in 1988 and return to power only after signaling that he would move back toward the center. Throughout the Western world, socialism seemed to be failing the pragmatic test, and some version of neoliberalism could easily seem the best hope of the left everywhere. In France, Mitterrand's own pullback was an instructive example. In Britain and Germany, ambitious young centrists would win the leadership of the major left-wing parties in the 1990s. Tony Blair and Gerhard Schröder looked, however, less to the example of their French counterpart than to Bill Clinton.

Clinton became the third neoliberal candidate the Democrats had nominated in five tries. His unsuccessful counterpart in 1988, Michael Dukakis, had been governor of Massachusetts. Like Carter, Dukakis and Clinton had managerial records as successful chief executives. All three had established personas that were mildly populist. All had to one degree or another put some daylight between themselves and powerful interest groups in their party. In terms of political savvy and campaigning skills, Clinton was far and away the most impressive. An obsessive policy wonk, chair of the neoliberal Democratic Leadership Council, he had established solid credentials as a politician of the "third way." His election brought hopes for an administration that somehow could fulfill the hopes of the Democratic left while defusing charges of statism and excessive spending. Two issues defined his failure in that respect.

Clinton had not hesitated to declare that his first priority as president would be to establish a national health plan—one that would avoid the pitfalls of top-down bureaucratic command and yet provide full medical care for everyone efficiently. Within eighteen months, an arduously developed administration plan lay in ruins, never having come to a vote in Congress. The Clinton health plan in effect lost the pragmatic argument on grounds of its fundamental nature (despite its complex organization, it was statist), likely efficiency (its multilayered character made it easy to parody), and cost. A self-styled moderate president had come across as attempting to implement a massive enlargement of government. In the mid-term elections, he lost control of Congress.

It was only after that debacle that Clinton moved to the right. In 1996, after considerable backing and filling, he not only accepted but embraced a mostly Republican-generated welfare reform program that rejected the ideal of permanent income maintenance for the jobless. Here, he most clearly stepped back from the entitlement ideal that had characterized the Great Society at its high point and had become a staple of European social democracy. Across the Atlantic, such a measure was still unthinkable. Clinton's reelection in 1996 transformed him from a failed president to a paragon of "third way" solutions. Six months later, Tony Blair led the "New Labour" party to Britain in England and set about to emulate the American president.

It remains unclear whether Clinton and Blair have been masters of innovative social policy or master political illusionists. There can be little doubt, however, that American and British electorates both approved of their retreat from an equalitarian, welfarist agenda. At the same time, the constituencies in both countries for activist programs of social benefits remained large. The political demographics of turn-of-the-century America had changed remarkably since the heyday of the Johnson presidency. Britain had gone through many of the same experiences. Many movements that seemed on the fringe at the beginning of the 1960s—the aspirations of people of color, feminism, gay liberation—had won wide mainstream assent. The rejection of traditional middle-class morality with regard to sex, marriage, and illegitimacy had become a commonplace aspect of everyday life. Organized labor, despite some efforts to return to its roots, drew less on a blue-collar working class and more on middle-class public employees. Senior citizens, as a group both the fastest growing and most affluent of the standard age segments in the population, had a stronger voice than ever before. The public policy intelligentsia, a novelty when Roosevelt drew on the "Brains Trust," had become an integral part of political life, churning out solutions to every conceivable problem.

All these groups wanted something from government, not a grand utopian makeover of society, but programs to meet specific needs: antidiscrimination regulations, affirmative action, income support, government assistance in efforts to expand union memberships and political power, protection of Social Security and Medicare, a prescription drug benefit, and the chance to develop and administer new social programs. The future of the American democratic left lay in a past that stretched back at least to World War I— incremental steps toward universal social benefits. The result might never be perfect equality, much less the abolition of private property, but it would move society in that direction. Much the same might be said of the European democratic left, except that in Europe the agenda was much farther along and the break with true socialist aspirations far from universal.

In both cases, the social-provision state faced major pragmatic problems. The European example seemed to demonstrate that huge social programs could not be paid for by redistributionist taxation. Rather they required heavy consumption taxes that affected rich and poor alike, thus undermining the goal of equalitarianism. The European social state also seemed to suck capital out of the private sector, place limits on economic growth, and thereby diminish increasing state income from taxation to pay for increasingly expensive social benefits. European social programs appeared overstressed—the once-admired British national health system was perhaps the most conspicuous example—and even more precarious in long-run financial stability than the U.S. Social Security system. In the United States as well as Europe, moreover, the left was no longer simply a movement for economic change based on materialist assumptions. Cultural radicalism jostled with economic radicalism, making coalition-building tricky.

In both America and Europe, the left clings to its fundamental premises: human nature is rational and beneficent, equality is the prime goal of social policy, the state is an indispensable tool for good. But more than ever its thinkers have made peace with the insights of classical liberalism: human nature is mixed, individual freedom and autonomy are incompatible with an equality imposed from above, the state is both a necessity and a limited tool for social improvement.

The future of the American (and European) left is most likely revealed by the history of the last several decades. Socialism, as once understood, is dead. Equality is not a goal to be flaunted. Large constituencies exist to support a movement that will give them state benefits. But big entitlement programs must face tests of workability and financial soundness; if they do not seem to pass, they will go the way of the Clinton health plan and their advocates likely will be less successful at hanging on than the resourceful Clinton.

The prospect for the American democratic left, then, is democratic politics—fighting out one issue at a time within an environment of strongly felt controversy, winning some, losing some, perhaps moving forward.

Ohio University

Notes

1. Stanley Baldwin, *This Torch of Freedom* (London, 1935), 3–6.
2. Norman Thomas article, *New York Times*, 18 June 1933.
3. In 1960, for example, a young British Labour activist, Betty Boothroyd, worked in the presidential campaign of John F. Kennedy; later elected to the House of Commons, she became its first female Speaker. In Britain's general election of 1997, noted American political consultants advised both Conservative and Labour campaign strategists.
4. John Kenneth Galbraith, *The Affluent Society* (Boston, 1958), chap. 23, 250.

5. Norman Thomas retired after the 1960 campaign. Thereafter, the Socialist party abstained from running presidential candidates. Functioning as an educational organization, it became in practical terms a caucus of policy advocates on the left wing of the Democratic party.

6. Gareth Davies, *From Opportunity to Entitlement: The Transformation and Decline of Great Society Liberalism* (Lawrence, Kan., 1996).

MARK WICKHAM-JONES

From Reformism to Resignation and Remedialism? Labour's Trajectory Through British Politics

On 9 April 1992, the British Labour party lost its fourth successive general election.[1] The outcome, coming after prolonged economic difficulties, led many commentators to call into question altogether the viability of the reformist project in the United Kingdom. For Labour's leaders, the result was bitterly disappointing. To lose any general election is, of course, evidence of failure. But, given the extent of the radical transformation the party appeared to have undergone in the late 1980s and early 1990s, to lose in the propitious circumstances of 1992 was especially frustrating. Just over five years later, however, much of the period under a new leader, Tony Blair, and having undergone further dramatic adaptation, including a comprehensive rebranding as "New Labour," the party not only took office at the general election of 1 May 1997 but won a landslide victory of 179 seats. A little over four years later it won a second landslide victory with a majority just 12 seats fewer at 167: it was an unparalleled achievement in the party's history.

To many observers, this remarkable electoral recovery came at a high price in terms of Labour's social democratic credentials.[2] They concluded that the cost of electoral victory was a shift from the reformism to which the party had adhered, albeit in an increasingly moderate and timid fashion, to a stance that could best be characterized, in the terms of Adam Przeworski, by its resignation and by its remedialism.[3] Resignation reflected New Labour's utter acceptance of the market economy and the forces of globalization. Remedialism reflected the sense that all that a left-wing government could do was tamper with the worst excesses of free-market capitalism. Such tinkering did not constitute a reformist program.

In this essay, I examine Labour's electoral recovery between 1992 and 2001 and I ask whether it has been achieved through the abandonment of any remaining social democratic ideological commitments. In the next section, I place Labour's electoral decline within a theoretical context. In the third section, focusing on economic strategy and welfare policy, I chart Labour's recovery after its 1992 defeat and summarize its record in office. I go on to outline the attempts by Tony Blair to provide theoretical underpinnings with which to define the New Labour project. Finally, I assess the extent to which New Labour may be considered reformist. As will be seen, the leitmotivs of reformism, resignation, and remedialism litter my discussion of Labour's trajectory through British politics over the last decade or so.

Theorizing Labour's Decline

Labour suffered four general-election defeats in a row between 1979 and 1992. In the aftermath of 1992, many were bleak about the party's prospects. David Butler and Denis Kavanagh argued, "At first sight [the result] seemed to confirm the rejection of socialism, as in many countries, and to show that the center-left had no clear and electorally attractive political message." They indicated that the election marked "a rejection of what was offered by Labour and raised again questions about the party's future as a party of government."[4] One group of scholars asked, "Can Labour win again in the foreseeable future? On the face of it there seems little reason for optimism." Their answer made miserable reading for the left: "But to reach the summit [win] would take an unprecedented effort even on the most optimistic assumptions about the electoral climate."[5] Peter Jenkins, a newspaper columnist, was caustic: "It was a reversal no less fundamental than in 1983 and in 1987, indeed a confirmation of the watershed that flowed from 1979. . . . Labour lost because it was Labour."[6] Of the party's decline, Crewe argued, "It may well not be fully reversible in the short term."[7] Unsurprisingly, those within the party were equally gloomy: "Labour's fourth successive defeat plunged the party into despair."[8]

Labour's difficulties were not confined to electoral matters.[9] In 1988, the party's membership had hit a record low of 267,000. It had risen by 1991 to around 320,000, but it is likely that the reported figure exaggerated the true level. Finances were equally problematic. In 1988 there was a deficit of £2 million: one-quarter of the party's staff at its London HQ was made redundant. But unsurprisingly, given the cost of national campaigning and advertising, Labour's finances remained parlous in 1992. Moreover, the party was overly dependent on its affiliated trade unions for financial support, a link that was politically awkward and electorally unpopular.

It is easy to understand why commentators were quite so pessimistic in 1992 about the reformist prospect in the United Kingdom. Their conclusions echoed theoretical arguments advanced more generally by a variety of scholars. Notably, Adam Przeworski exposed the structural and electoral constraints confronting social democratic actors.[10] The structural constraints concerned the nature of the capitalist system within which social democrats sought office and attempted to implement reformist programs. Przeworski summarized the argument: "Structural dependence theory asserts that the private ownership of productive assets imposes constraints which are so binding that no government, regardless of what its objectives might be, can pursue policies adverse to interests of capitalists."[11] Through globalization and the greater mobility of capital, such constraints were intensified. Governments must ensure a healthy economy as a prerequisite for any other goals. In a private system, this means meeting the policy preferences of employers. Accordingly, it is the latter that replace the aspirations of social democrats in determining an administration's programmatic outlook. The implication of this conclusion is that any government must hold down taxation rates and curb public spending. A dégringolade will be the outcome if governments do not accept this situation and persist in pursuing radical measures.

Przeworski is not alone in articulating such ideas. By the mid-1970s, the centerpiece of many social democratic reformist initiatives, the welfare state was no longer acknowledged by many scholars to be a solution to economic difficulties as had been the case but rather was identified as a direct and significant cause of them. Social democratic administrations ran into trouble throughout much of Northern Europe as previously successful policy tools failed (most obviously those of Keynesian demand management and currency devaluations). By the late 1980s, the structural dependency thesis was a commonly held one. Perry Anderson noted, "The tightening of constraints reduces the objective space for its traditional policies."[12]

Jonathan Moses was equally frank, "The environment has changed in such a way that traditional social democratic instruments are no longer effective."[13] I have outlined the structural constraints thesis at some length because, as will be seen, the arguments with which Tony Blair and other senior figures within New Labour justify the party's policy outlook resonate many of its features.

The electoral constraints identified by Przeworski were no less daunting than the structural ones. Academics have long asserted that the search for office leads social democrats to look for allies outside their traditional working-class base. Przeworski concluded that this search was fatally comprised: as parties move to the center, they dilute their class appeal and lose votes among their traditional supporters. Scholars noted that the bases of support underpinning social democratic parties had been eroded by a number of factors: de-industrialization, the declining numbers of manual workers, and the fragmentation in identity and in defining characteristics of those remaining members of the working class.[14] Not all academics were as pessimistic as Przeworski, but many indicated that reformists face formidable electoral difficulties in generating sufficient support to win office. Most obvious, of course, was the argument that office can only be won through a wholesale dilution of reformism.

Labour's Recovery

Clearly identified with Labour's modernizing wing of the party, Tony Blair became leader of the Labour party in July 1994, following the unexpected death of John Smith. Blair's diagnosis of electoral failure was stark. Labour had lost in 1992 because it had failed to make the necessary changes to its policy outlook, organization, and electoral structure. Under his leadership, it would.

In the three years to May 1997, significant changes were made to the party's policy commitments, electoral strategy, and organization. Especially important developments were made to Labour's economic policy and to its approach to welfare issues.[15] As shadow chancellor, Gordon Brown was given the task of redefining the party's economic policy. His conclusion was that the party's economic policy (and in particular its "shadow budget" of March 1992 outlining modest tax rises) was a significant cause of electoral defeat. Although the proposed increase in taxation was mild, its threshold coincided with the aspirations of upwardly mobile voters. In any case, over

half the electorate thought that their taxation would rise and opposed the change.

Under Blair, Clause IV of the constitution, Labour's historic
commitment to public ownership, was dropped. In its place, the party
endorsed the profit-making activities of the private sector. In May
1995, Blair committed Labour to the goal of low inflation above all
other economic targets and painted a bleak picture of the options
available to a reformist government. A repeated rhetorical claim
made by both Blair and his shadow chancellor was that they had
decisively broken with the policies of "tax and spend" that had characterized the party's approach in 1992.[16] For a long time the party
hesitated over any changes in taxation, the issue that had apparently then done so much damage. In January 1997, Brown stated
that there would be no increases in personal taxation rates during
the first term of a Labour administration: the top tax rate would stay
at the level inherited from the Conservatives: 40 percent. The promise was described as a "conclusive break" with Labour's past.[17] One
commentator argued that the pledge spelled "not simply the end of
socialism but of social democracy."[18] Brown announced that, during
its first two years of office, the new Labour government would accept the public spending levels previously established by the Conservatives. Many doubted the realism of this pledge given the
implausibility of the existing plans.

The changes to Labour's welfare policy mirrored those to its
economic strategy. In April 1992 two commitments had been at the
center of the party's manifesto: promises to increase spending on
old-age pensions and on child benefits. Both were universal, offered
respectively, without qualification, to the old and to those with children. The proposals were typical of Labour's approach to welfare,
according to which it was assumed that the state should provide
universally a wide range of benefits as a right to citizens. If nothing
else, such benefits were a means of tackling poverty. To Labour modernizers, such promises were symptomatic of what was wrong with
the party's outlook.[19]

By 1997, Labour offered a different approach to welfare. The
party retreated from any broad commitment to universal benefits
provided as rights of citizenship. Some benefits, they argued, should
be targeted directly upon the most needy. The new approach was
underpinned by a shift in Labour's philosophical outlook. Blair placed
emphasis on "responsibility": any rights or entitlements that were
to be enjoyed by citizens were to be matched by obligations. On

welfare reform, Blair promised new and original solutions to apparently intractable problems: new Labour would "think the unthinkable." Welfare reform would be "one of the fundamental objectives" of his administration.[20]

By 1997, Blair appeared to have solved the party's difficulties in terms of membership and finance. The year before he became leader, individual party membership had stood at 266,00 and was falling. As a result of a huge recruitment drive, membership topped 400,000 in 1996. The party's finances remained precarious with a small deficit in 1995 and larger ones in 1996 and 1997 (unsurprising in the run-up to the election). But Labour diversified the revenue sources upon which it relied. In 1986 trade unions had provided 76 percent of the party's income (fund-raising a mere 6 percent). A decade later, the union share was down to 45 percent and fund-raising up to 37 percent.[21]

In May 1997, Labour won a crushing electoral victory. At 10.3 percent, the swing between the two main parties was a postwar record as the Conservatives lost half their seats in parliaments. Especially dramatic was Labour's share of those too young to vote in 1992 (57 percent) and of those who had abstained in that election (55 percent).[22] For Blair, victory marked the end of the first phase of New Labour: "becoming a modern social democratic party fit for government."[23]

Several points should be noted about the election victory. First, the extent and originality of the changes to Labour's structure and policy program after 1994 should not be exaggerated. Earlier developments were made during the 1980s and early 1990s. Many subsequent reforms built on these developments in an evolutionary fashion and were neither as dramatic nor as innovative as had been claimed.[24] Second, it is by no means certain what role the creation of "New Labour" played in the general-election outcome. The key event during the 1992–97 parliament was 16 September 1992, so-called Black Wednesday. The United Kingdom was ejected from membership from the European Exchange Rate Mechanism (ERM) as a result of the government's failure to defend overvalued sterling against currency market speculation. Black Wednesday had an immediate impact on electoral perceptions. The economy had been one of the Conservatives' strongest cards. But, when asked which party was better able to handle Britain's economic difficulties, the Conservatives trailed Labour from September 1992 until May 1997. The rebranding of the party as New Labour was important: Brown and Blair successfully projected an image of Labour as a moderate party. But the legacy of Black Wednesday broke decisively the Conservatives' claim to the party of economic competence.

Once in office, Labour's leaders followed a cautious line in terms of economic policy. By 2001, two economic storms had been weathered: the inheritance of an overheating economy and the Far East Asian crisis of 1998. Inflation had remained low, declining to its lowest level since the 1960s, while the fall in unemployment was equally impressive (dropping below one million for the first time since 1975). Growth averaged 2.9 percent and the public finances shifted into surplus. Blair's government appeared to have refuted the charge that Labour could never manage the economy effectively.[25]

As chancellor, Gordon Brown placed considerable emphasis on economic stability. He handed over operational control of monetary policy to a newly independent Bank of England. The decision was an indication of the emphasis Labour placed on attaining low inflation and the difficulties in finding a credible route to that goal. It was undoubtedly the single most important economic act taken by Labour during the first term, one that was widely welcomed by financial markets. Many commentators concluded that the Bank's monetary-policy committee played an important part in securing a low level of price increases between 1997 and 2001.

Brown complemented this approach to monetary policy with a tough line over fiscal matters. The decision to keep to Conservative spending targets was complimented by a range of tax increases covering many areas of the economy (but not personal income tax), the most dramatic of which abolished tax credits on dividends. The overall impact of these increases, characterized as stealth taxes because they had no direct impact on take-home incomes, was that the state of public finances improved markedly (helped by a buoyant economy and underspending). The Comprehensive Spending Review in July 2000 heralded something of a change in direction for Labour with increases in expenditure (£43 billion over several years), mainly for capital investment. Health and education were the main beneficiaries.

The Blair administration sought to reduce unemployment, partly through its New Deal program, which prepared young people for the labor market and found them subsidized work either in the private sector or one of a number of other options. Brown also introduced measures to integrate the tax and benefit system, thus eliminating the poverty trap where people were better off on benefits than in low-paid work. The most important of these was 1998's Working Families Tax Credit (WFTC).

The issue of welfare reform was placed at the center of Labour's agenda on entering office. Frank Field was explicitly appointed as minister for welfare reform, only to resign in the first reshuffle in 1998. His experience was emblematic of the difficulties the issue was to encounter: promising grand reforms, New Labour's rhetoric was out of alignment with the realities confronting fundamental policy development. In 1999, the administration's welfare reform and pensions bill was greeted with hyperbole: "The new regime will be far tougher than people thought. . . . We will end the something-for-nothing approach that has characterised the past."[26] Blair was equally theatrical, calling the bill "a fundamental break with the past" and stating, "The days of an automatic right to benefit will go."[27] Though some regulations were intensified, the practical impact of the legislation was by no means immediately obvious.

Labour's record in economic management paid a direct popular dividend. Between May 1997 and June 2001, Labour dominated the economic argument in a straightforward and transparent fashion. For every month of the administration, bar one, those polled on economic credibility favored the government over the Conservative opposition. There appeared to be a clear link between the electorate's attitude to the management of the economy and its voting intention: the two moved closely together, with, for the most part, Labour enjoying a stronger lead in the latter than it did in the former.

New Labour's first term in office culminated in a second land-slide election victory in June 2001: the party's majority, at 167, was barely dented in a small swing of 1.8 percent to the Conservatives.[28] The result was unsurprising: for the first time, an administration had led the polls throughout the parliament. Labour lost only seven seats (and captured two). For Blair, the result marked the culmination of the second phase of New Labour, "to use our 1997 victory to put in place the foundations that would allow us to change the country in a way that lasts."[29]

The Coherence of New Labour

At times between 1994 and 2001, Blair appeared to be stung by the charge that the New Labour project lacked coherence and a principled underpinning. The absence of a foundation left the party open to charges of being opportunistic. In such circumstances, Blair turned to the "Third Way." The bland, elliptical phrase was revealing, a reflection of the uncertainty surrounding the Labour leader's attempt to define his project. Blair deployed the term in a variety of contexts. He used the term to distinguish his proposals from those of the corporatist and neoliberalist economic policies that had shaped postwar Britain.[30] He used it to locate Labour between the traditions of the European and American political economy, and he claimed that the Third Way marked a distinction between individualism and collectivism.[31] Speaking in Paris, the prime minister declared that it comprised, among other features, an emphasis on solidarity and tolerance.[32] Later these features were dropped. In their place democracy, mutual obligation, internationalism, equal worth, and responsibility were added to liberty, opportunity, community, and justice.[33] To critics, Blair's values were anodyne and unremarkable: they had little to do with those traditionally associated with social democracy. His insistence that the values of the Third Way were those that Labour had held in the past and that it was simply the means that had changed did little to reassure critics who saw the construct as pragmatic.

Academics, most notably Anthony Giddens, picked up on the Third Way.[34] Giddens's version was as rhetorical as that of the prime minister: it was by no means obvious what guidance it gave about the direction of public policy. This elusiveness was matched by radical but sweeping expressions. Perhaps surprisingly, few politicians followed Blair. Robin Cook, the foreign secretary, gave a few bland speeches articulating the phrase. A few other, junior members of the government promoted the phrase; it was not adopted by Gordon Brown, whose outlook at the Treasury was relentlessly matter-of-fact. Outside the United Kingdom there was some interest in the Third Way. A shared interest in it was a small part of the close relationship that Tony Blair enjoyed with U.S. President Bill Clinton. In 1999, a joint publication between Gerhard Schröder and the British prime minister outlined a common commitment to it (though little of substance came of it).[35] Others, notably Lionel Jospin, the French prime minister, were much less positive.

The Third Way fizzled out. On occasion it reappeared, usually in a rather half-hearted and uncertain fashion. Blair was unrepentant. In May 2002, he claimed, "The whole concept of the third way is really revised from the same set of beliefs; that the Labour party stands for certain values, community, opportunity to all, especially from all, a belief in social justice, but that these beliefs should be translated into the world in a different way for today. I have never changed my beliefs on these things." Following the evaporation of the Third Way, the notion that Labour required a coherent philosophy persisted. At the end of the first term, the issue of "public service reform" emerged. Blair's approach to the matter was straightforward (and could be described as classic Third Way).

The issue was not new. In July 1999, to a private-sector audience, Blair was scathing about the public sphere, "You try getting change in the public sector and public services—I bear the scars in my back after two years in government."[36] A year later he told *The Observer*, "It is far harder to change the way a public service works because it doesn't have the great engine that the market is always creating for change in the private sector. You don't want the health service to be turned into a market place, but you've got to look at ways of pioneering change."[37] In June 2001, public-sector reform was given new significance. Blair argued, "I think that breaking down the barriers between public, private and voluntary sectors will carry on. . . . We've got to break through this debilitating choice between old-style socialism and ultra-Thatcherism."[38] He continued, "We must be a reforming government as well as simply an investing one" and asserted that public-sector reform would be "hugely important." He claimed that it marked the third phase of New Labour: "It is about driving forward reforms, building lasting change—and a better society—on the foundations so carefully laid."[39]

As with the Third Way, the notion of public-service reform was characterized by its uncertain nature. Again pragmatism was a defining feature. In October 2001, Blair stated, "We have also been held back by ideological clashes, going back decades, which have distracted from the real challenge of improving our public services."[40] He asserted, "We have become the pragmatic party, pursuing perfectly idealistic objectives in a measured and non-dogmatic way."[41] Of the controversial Private Finance Initiative (the contractual involvement of private firms in public-sector projects), he stated, "Where it works and delivers a better public service, use it; where it doesn't, don't."[42]

Critics charged that the initiative amounted to a form of privatization, a charge Blair vehemently denied. He claimed, "Nobody's talking about privatising public services."[44] He went on, "There shouldn't be an ideological barrier to providing better public services. That's not the same as privatising the public services." Blair noted that public-sector pay rates and employment levels were up and gave four sweeping principles underpinning his initiative: national standards and accountability; flexibility, innovation, and devolution; changed conditions of employment; and increased choice.[45] Specific criticisms were made of increased private-sector involvement in the public sector concerning such matters as the distribution of risk and profit as well as the terms of service for those working in such areas (pension rights was a particular point of concern). Roy Hattersley made a general point: "The basic philosophy [of public service reform] is unclear. It may be that it doesn't have a basic philosophy. . . . If you read his speech today there isn't a political idea running through it. He said he believes in fairness. We all believe in fairness."[46]

New Labour's Abandonment of Social Democracy: Resignation and Remedialism

New Labour's discourse is littered with a sense of resignation and an indication that remedial, paternal interventionism is the most that social democrats can hope for in the current climate. Many of Blair's and Brown's speeches echo Przeworski's contention of structural dependency. Both have placed special emphasis on the impact globalization has had upon the reformist project.[47] Blair argued bluntly: "Globalization has destroyed any notion of countries cutting themselves off from world markets. Go-it-alone reflation or spending policies will be mercilessly and immediately punished by capital markets that can overthrow a nation's currency."[48] He went on to claim, "The Keynesian post war consensus is over."[49] In a similar vein, Brown asserted, "Today, unlike 20 years ago, no national government can set tax, spending and borrowing policies in isolation. They do so within a competitive global economy where they have to borrow and to justify their policies for expenditure and taxation."[50] Blair was stark: "We live in a global economy today. We compete in that or we fail."[51] He told the French Assembly, "In the end none of our nations can compete in the old way."[52]

Labour's approach indicates that there are structural limits to the level of state spending in an economy. Blair's joint statement with Gerhard Schröder stated that "public expenditure as a proportion of national income has more or less reached the limits of acceptability. Constraints on 'tax and spend' force radical modernization of the public sector and reform of the public services to achieve better value for money."[53] Blair and Brown also imply that there are structural limits to the levels at which taxation rates can be set.[54] In 1997, the shadow chancellor pronounced, "How governments tax sends clear signals about the economic activities they believe should be encouraged, and indeed discouraged, and the values they want to entrench in society."[55] In 2001, Blair stated: "You have to be extremely careful nowadays [about tax], particularly with the very top earners, you know, the international market in which most of them work."[56] Another feature of New Labour's resignation has been its acceptance of inequalities. Blair told *The Guardian* frankly, "Yes, but even making allowance for that [the need to tackle poverty], inequalities have merit.'"[57]

New Labour's endorsement of the private sector is, in general terms at any rate, explicit. Blair was straightforward: "I certainly believe that where there is no overriding reason for preferring the public provision of goods and services, particularly where those services operate in a competitive market, then the presumption should be that economic activity is best left to the private sector, with market forces being fully encouraged to operate."[58] He continued, "I accept the need for economic discipline, and embrace the role of free enterprise in the economy. There will be no retreat from any of that." He was able to conclude, "New Labour is now the party of business." Such sentiments have often been repeated in office: "A framework that allows market forces to work properly is essential to economic success."[59]

A sense of resignation permeated much of New Labour's economic policy stance on entering office. When the Japanese company Fujitsu closed a factory in his Sedgefield constituency, Blair argued bluntly: "It would be totally dishonest to pretend government can prevent such decisions . . . let us not kid ourselves. In certain sectors there will be an impact. . . . We can't as the government do much about the twists and turns of world markets in an increasingly globalised economy."[60] He told the PES Congress in Malmö, Sweden: "The public simply won't pay more taxes and spend more to fund an unreconstructed welfare system."[61] The speech went on to claim, melodramatically, "We modernise or die."

What impact did Blair and Brown's resignation have on Labour's policy program? From one perspective, as Przeworski's framework indicates, it left them with little more than a modest remedialism. (Arguably, of course, this remedialism predated Blair: in 1991, Anderson concluded Labour to offer "essentially a more generous level of social provision.")[62] Certainly, the rhetoric of remedialism permeates many of Blair's speeches.[63] A frequent theme concerns the need to protect the weak and the disadvantaged: "For 18 years the poorest people in our country have been forgotten by government. . . . I want that to change."[64] A few months later, Blair told *Time*, "The British feel a very strong sense of compassion and social unity."[65] In a constituency speech, he concluded, "We believe in the responsibility to help those who are in genuine need, unable to look after themselves."[66] He told one audience that "at the root of it all [New Labour] is a simple belief in fairness. It isn't fair that people are held back or live in poverty. We want to change it."[67]

Blair's commitment to paternalism and remedialism stood in contrast to his persistent refusal to endorse redistributive and egalitarian policies, measures commonly associated with the social democratic tradition. During a 2001 interview, Jeremy Paxman asked Blair, on eleven occasions, whether the increased gap between rich and poor in the United Kingdom was acceptable. He refused to answer.

At times, Blair and Brown's rhetoric appeared to eschew even the most modest of remedialisms, most obviously perhaps in the discourse that they articulated over welfare. Their emphasis on work and individualism was especially indicative in this regard. In June 1997, Blair argued, "In the absence of clear philosophy of rights and duties, the welfare system can discourage hard work and honesty. . . . It locks people into dependency on benefits."[68] In similar vein, Brown asserted, "The welfare state discourages work and by creating barriers to work prevents people from being independent."[69] Blair told a U.S. audience, "Painful and difficult though it is, we are going to reform the welfare state, cutting dependence, getting the help to those that really need it."[70] There is much in this discourse, manifestly, that is utterly at odds with the social democratic tradition.

New Labour's Espousal of Social Democracy: Reformism and Redistribution

New Labour's break with reformism is, however, not as complete as the above section might indicate. On occasion, though not often, Blair's rhetoric is ambiguous. When pushed about his refusal to discuss inequality, Blair responded, "You know the Labour Party stands for a more equal society. I prefer myself to concentrate on how we give a better standard of living to people who are on middle and low incomes which is exactly what we are trying to do."[71] Asked whether narrowing inequalities was one of the government's goals, he was unequivocal: "Yes, of course, it is."

Disentangling New Labour's discourse from its policy measures highlights the complexity of its ideological commitments. New Labour's rhetoric appears at odds with any principle of redistribution. But many of Gordon Brown's measures (and arguably the overall thrust of his strategy) are less obviously out of alignment with an egalitarianism goal. The WFTC, for example, offers an automatic top-up to those on low incomes and goes to around one million families: for some, it represents a huge increase in pay.[72] The redistributive intent of Labour's economic strategy should not, therefore, be neglected.

Whether such measures take Labour from a remedial to a redistributive outlook is an open question. Between 1997 and 2001, the overall impact of Brown's budgets was redistributive: benefits were channeled so that the worst off gained while the better off paid more, though not that much more, in tax.[73] In 2000, Andrew Dilnot acclaimed the pre-budget report proposals as especially generous: "These are very, very substantial changes. It really is a dramatic change. . . . I can't think of any economic measure giving such a large group of the population gains on this scale in 20 years of tax and benefits policy."[74] Figures from the Institute for Fiscal Studies indicated an income gain of 10 percent for those in the poorest tenth of the population (higher for particular categories within that group), while for the top tenth the gain was just one percent. For John Hills, it amounted to "redistribution by stealth."[75]

In March 2002, the first budget of Labour's second term was dramatic. Breaking the spirit but not the fine print of his 2001 promise not to raise income tax, Brown increased national insurance (a covert kind of income tax, of which for most taxpayers it represents a form) for employees and employers in order to direct extra resources to the National Health Service. He also froze tax allowances. Many commentators concluded that Brown's decision marked a significant change in trajectory: "It was perhaps the boldest and clearest reassertion of social democracy to be heard since the 1970s from the front bench in the House of Commons."[76] Peter Riddell concluded that the budget "confirms the Blair government's credentials as social democrats. After the caution and stealth taxes of the first term, the Chancellor of the Exchequer has produced a distinctively Labour budget with redistributive tax measures and big increases in public spending."[77] *The Times* headline captured well the sense of a change in direction: "Chancellor gambles career on 'tax-and-spend' strategy." For *The Guardian*, "Brown bets all on the NHS."[78]

For some, the scale of Labour's redistributive imperative was inadequate: they insisted the administration was a neoliberal one. Regarding much of New Labour's rhetoric, it is hard to quibble with such a verdict. In other areas judgment is more complex. As noted above, there was a redistributive aspect to it. For all of Brown's disavowals, there remained an element of traditional-style "tax and spend" in many of Labour's measures. For confirmation of this point, look at the tax changes, the comprehensive spending review, and the 2002 budget. Aspects of the strategy were interventionist, seeking to correct endemic market failures and shape the decisions of the private sector (in much the same way that social democrats did in the 1950s and 1960s). Noteworthy aspects of the government's strategy, most notably the use of tax credits and the New Deal, were indicative of a different, non-neoliberal approach. Blair's rhetoric rejected the notion that governments could intervene. But the New Deal and tax credits presumed market failure to be all-pervasive. When the firm BMW moved to close a large car factory at Longbridge in Birmingham, the government was quick to offer aid.

The difficulty of assessing Labour's reformist credentials is heightened by the fact that the gap between rich and poor widened during Labour's first term, essentially the result of economic growth benefiting the better-off disproportionately, making the United Kingdom a less equal society.[79]

Conclusions

I have sought to highlight some of the complexities and ambiguities surrounding New Labour. A sense of resignation and remedialism permeates much of the Blair administration's outlook and its rhetoric. But the party's commitment to modest reformism and redistribution should not be ignored. From this perspective, Przeworski's model of resignation and remedialism should not be applied in a rigid fashion. For example, there have been tensions between business and Labour that his framework would not lead us to expect (over the 2002 budget, regulation, mergers, taxation, and electronic mail).

Neoliberal strategic pressures, a convergence of a market-oriented policy regime, have not hemmed in New Labour's economic decisions. Przeworski accepts such an outcome: "The margin of manoeuvre may be very narrow with regard to some policies but broad with regard to other policies."[80]

In conclusion, two significant points follow. First, in the analysis of New Labour, it is important to separate the rhetoric and discourse from policy and to disconnect both from outcomes. Moreover, there is a sense in which New Labour should be not characterized as a monolithic entity projecting a single identity. Aspects of the party's outlook remain unresolved and ill defined—something reflected in the administration's ability for the most part to hold together the diverse coalition that elected it to office. Blair and Brown (especially Brown) have been able to articulate different ideas in different contexts to a diverse range of audiences. Accordingly Labour may be both remedial and redistributive in its ideological alignment. This arrangement may be most apparent in Brown's redistributive agenda coupled with his pursuit of economic stability.

Second, to the extent that New Labour's outlook is social democratic, it is apparent that changes have been made to the traditional reformist program. These developments are clear in welfare and in economic strategy. Brown's measures remain redistributive and interventionist, but the emphasis placed on work as the means to secure a more equal society is at odds with past reliance upon benefits. Often his initiatives are targeted, and in areas such as the New Deal they are, arguably at any rate, coercive and illiberal. These are features of New Labour's project that, for reasons of space and as a result of my use of Przeworski's framework, I have not discussed. Labour's construction of a "new social democracy" owes much to its preparedness to impose contractual arrangements upon segments of the population. As such, illiberalism may be as much a defining feature of the new social democratic outlook in the United Kingdom as the concepts discussed above: resignation, remedialism, redistribution, and reformism.

How permanent is Labour's electoral dominance likely to be? Any judgment on this issue needs to be read with caution: remember the verdicts passed on Labour's defeat in 1992. Events can move swiftly out of an administration's control. A few points can be noted. First, the events of September 1992 and its immediate aftermath, when the United Kingdom left the ERM, have shaped British politics decisively. They marked a new alignment between party popularity and economic competence upon which Labour was able to build in office between 1997 and 2001.

Second, the extent to which the origins of New Labour go back further into the party's history than to Blair's election as leader in July 1994 gives an indication of the resources that have been deployed in restructuring the party's outlook. It took a great deal of wherewithal and effort, as well as a series of election defeats, to establish Labour as a different kind of reformist party. Achieving credibility, signaling the extent of the changes to the electorate, and securing voters' trust was a time-consuming and complex process. Losing such trust might be a swift matter, but arguably the character of Labour's changes has provided the basis for the party to achieve some sort of hegemonic dominance in British politics. In this sense, though doubts persist about its ideological substance, New Labour is not a shallow construct: over nearly two decades, the party's transformation led to important reforms becoming embedded in its structure and outlook. There are, of course, reasons to doubt New Labour's capacity to secure hegemony, but equally Crewe has argued that the party's cross-class appeal, its domination of the center ground, and its political competence and institutional support give reason to conclude that it might prove to be an enduring political phenomenon.[81]

Third, New Labour has been helped in the establishment of such a trajectory by the utter disarray of the Conservative opposition (about which no more can be said for reasons of space, but which persists at the time of writing).

Fourth, much remains uncertain about what Blair envisages to be the Labour party's long-term future. At times, he has hinted that he would like to see a much more formal arrangement with the generally left-inclined Liberal Democrats. Arguably a pact or a merger between the two would seal Labour's hegemony over British politics. Equally many within Labour would resist such a course.

Problems continue to confront the party. Blair has not solved either its financial difficulties or secured a buoyant membership. Attempting to diversify its income base away from its affiliated trade unions led Labour to seek and accept donations from the business sector. It soon became apparent that such donations might create conflicts of interest. In 1998 the party returned a donation of one million pounds from Bernie Ecclestone when it was revealed that motor racing, a sport with which he was associated, had benefited from a change of policy regarding tobacco advertising. Other donations were criticized on such grounds. A further problem concerned the suitability of donors such as Richard Desmond, a publisher of pornography who gave the party £100,000 in 2001.[82] Disagreements over government policy led some trade unions, such as the GMB and the railway workers, to cut their remaining funding of the party. These decisions left the party's finances in a parlous state.[83] By 2002, the government was inching its way toward state finance for political parties: the electorate proved hostile to the proposal.

Sustaining the party's increased membership proved equally difficult. Once elected to office, members drifted away at a steady rate. By 2002, Labour's individual membership stood at 280,000, a collapse of around 10 percent on the previous year.

Some policy issues remain unresolved. Brown's spending plans may require tax increases in the future if economic growth falters and the Treasury's revenue base falls. Should tax increases be required a few years from now, the electoral cycle may be out of kilter with the economic cycle, a situation that might damage Labour's popular support. The government must make a decision about British membership in a European monetary union at some stage in the near future, a decision that will have significant consequences for the Blair project.

Overall, however, the gradual entrenchment of Labour's transformation is indicative of a party that has become embedded within the British political system as a distinct entity. To that extent, Old Labour no longer exists in the consciousness of the British electorate.

University of Bristol

Notes

1. I am extremely grateful to Erwin Hargrove and Desmond King. All responsibility is mine.

2. Ivor Crewe, "The Thatcher Legacy," in Anthony King, *Britain at the Polls 1992* (Chatham, N.J., 1992), 1–28, 25; Colin Hay, *The Political Economy of New Labour* (Manchester, 1999), 58; Leo Panitch and Colin Leys, *The End of Parliamen- tary Socialism* (London, 1997), 4 and 259.

3. I take my title from Adam Przeworski: "I think I foresaw correctly their [social democrats'] ideological dynamic from revolution to reformism, to remedialism, to resignation," *European Consortium for Political Research News*, 2001, 32. Revolution has never really been part of British Labour's ideological program: hence its absence here. In more recent work, Przeworski has developed this theme: "The long-term historical evolution of social democracy proceeded from revolution to reformism to remedialism. The question remains is whether it will end in resignation"; see "How Many Ways Can Be Third?" in Andrew Glyn, ed., *Social Democracy in Neoliberal Times* (Oxford, 2001), 312–33, 316. Note that Przeworski's periodization does not match mine precisely.

4. David Butler and Denis Kavanagh, *The British General Election of 1992* (Basingstoke, 1992), 282–83.

5. Anthony Heath, Roger Jowell, and John Curtice, ed., *Labour's Last Change* (Aldershot, 1994), 275 and 280.

6. Peter Jenkins, *Anatomy of Decline* (London, 1996), 236.

7. Ivor Crewe, "Labour Force Changes, Working-Class Decline, and the Labour Vote in Postwar Britain," in Frances Fox Piven, *Labor Parties in Postindustrial Societies* (Oxford, 1991), 20–46, 23.

8. Butler and Kavanagh, *The British General Election of 1992*, 275.

9. Ibid., 59.

10. See Adam Przeworski, *Capitalism and Social Democracy* (Cambridge, 1985). I focus upon Przeworski's account because of its importance within that corpus and its relevance to the British case.

11. Adam Przeworski, *The State and the Economy Under Capitalism* (New York, 1991), 92.

12. Perry Anderson, "Introduction," in P. Anderson and P. Camiller, *Mapping the West European Left* (London, 1994), 1–22, 14.

13. Jonathan Moses, "Abdication from National Policy Autonomy: What's Left to Leave?" *Politics and Society* 22, no. 2 (June 1994): 125–48, at 133.

14. Perry Anderson noted "differences in work, income and security, age, gender, origin"; "Introduction," 14.

15. Mark Wickham-Jones, "How the Conservatives Lost the Economic Argument," in Andrew Geddes and Jonathon Tonge, eds., *Labour's Landslide* (Manchester, 1997), 100–118.

16. Tony Blair, speech, CPU conference, Cape Town, South Africa, 14 October 1996, 6; and Tony Blair, speech, Corn Exchange, London, 7 April 1997.

17. *Financial Times*, 24 January 1997.

18. P. Wintour, *The Observer*, 26 January 1997.

19. Paul Thompson, "Labour—The Natural Party of Opposition?" *Renewal* 1, no. 1 (1993): 1–10, at 3.

20. Tony Blair, speech, Singapore, January 1996.

21. Labour party, *NEC report* (1996 and 1997).

22. David Denver, "The Results: How Britain Voted (or Didn't)," in Andrew Geddes and Jonathan Tonge, eds., *Labour's Landslide*, 2–21.

23. Tony Blair, speech, LSE, 12 March 2002.

24. Martin Westlake, *Neil Kinnock* (London, 2001).

25. Mark Wickham-Jones, "Exorcising Ghosts," in Andrew Geddes and Jonathan Tonge, eds., *Labour's Second Landslide* (Manchester, 2001), 103–22.

26. Alistair Darling, "We Make No Apologies for Our Tough Welfare Regime," *The Independent*, 10 February 1999.

27. Tony Blair, "It Really Is the End of the Something for Nothing Days," *The Daily Mail*, 10 February 1999.

28. Denver, "The Results: How Britain Voted (or Didn't)," 9–24.

29. Tony Blair, speech, LSE, 12 March 2002.

30. Tony Blair, speech, London, 6 April 1997.

31. Tony Blair, speech, The Hague, 20 January 1998.

32. Tony Blair, speech, Paris, 24 March 1998.

33. Tony Blair, *The Third Way* (London, 1998).

34. Anthony Giddens, *The Third Way* (Oxford, 1998).

35. Tony Blair and Gerhard Schröder, "The Third Way/Die Neue Mitte," reproduced in Bodo Hombach, *The Politics of the New Centre* (Oxford, 2000), 157–77.

36. John Rentoul, *Tony Blair, Prime Minister* (London, 2002), 533.

37. He continued, "The public sector is still incredibly inflexible." Interview, *Observer*, 5 September 1999.

38. Transcript, *Observer*, 13 May 2001.

39. Tony Blair, speech, LSE, 12 March 2002.

40. Tony Blair, speech, 16 October 2001.

41. *The Guardian*, 29 May 2001.

42. Transcript, *The Guardian*, 11 September 2001.

43. Tony Blair, draft speech, TUC, 11 September 2001.

44. Transcript, *The Guardian*, 11 September 2001.

45. Employment conditions were dropped for Prime Minister's Office of Public Services Reform, *Reforming Our Public Services* (London, 2002), 3.

46. BBC Newsnight, 12 March 2002. Hattersley praised Blair's use of the word "equality."

47. A contrast with Przeworski, whose emphasis is on capital, domestic and international, rather than globalization.

48. Tony Blair, speech, 14 October 1996, 5; Tony Blair, speech, 22 May 1995.

49. Tony Blair, speech, Corn Exchange, London, 7 April 1997.

50. Gordon Brown, "Responsibility in Public Finance," 20 January 1997, 3.

51. Tony Blair, speech, IPPR, January 1997.

52. Tony Blair, speech, Paris, 24 March 1998.

53. Blair and Schröder, "The Third Way/Die Neue Mitte," 164.

54. Ibid., 167.

55. Brown, "Responsibility in Public Finance," 9.

56. Transcript, *The Guardian*, 11 September 2001.

57. Ibid.

58. Tony Blair, speech, Corn Exchange, London, 7 April 1997.

59. Blair and Schröder, "The Third Way/Die Neue Mitte," 166–67.

60. *The Times*, 17 September 1998.

61. Tony Blair, speech, Malmö, Sweden, June 1997, 3.

62. Perry Anderson, "The Light of Europe," in *English Questions* (London, 1991), 346.

63. Tony Blair, speech, CPU conference, Cape Town, South Africa, 14 October 1996, 9.

64. Tony Blair, speech, Aylesbury estate, Southwark, 2 June 1997, 1.

65. *Time*, 27 October 1997.

66. Tony Blair, speech, 20 December 1997, 4.

67. Tony Blair, speech, LSE, 12 March 2002.

68. Tony Blair, speech, Aylesbury estate, Southwark, 2 June 1997.

69. Gordon Brown, speech, 22 October 1996, 4.

70. Tony Blair, "New Britain," speech, 14 April 1998.

71. Transcript, *The Guardian*, 11 September 2001.

72. IFS, Green Budget report 2001 (London), 3.

73. H. Immervoll et al., "Budgeting for Fairness," mimeo, Department of Applied Economics, Cambridge, 1999, 8.

74. *The Guardian*, 10 November 2000.

75. John Hills, "How Labour Is Doing Good by Stealth for the Poor," *The Independent*, 4 June 2000.

76. Anatole Kaletsky, *The Times*, 18 April 2002.

77. *The Times*, 18 April 2002.

78. *The Guardian*, 18 April 2002.

79. *The Independent*, 14 July 2001.

80. Przeworski, "How Many Ways Can Be Third?" 330.

81. Ivor Crewe, "A New Political Hegemony," in A. King, ed., *Britain at the Polls, 2001* (London, 2002), 207–32

82. *The Guardian*, 29 May 2002.

83. *The Guardian*, 1 August 2001.

DAVID S. BELL

French Socialists: Refusing the "Third Way"

In 1997 the French Socialist party, in alliance with the small parties of the Communists, Verts (left-wing ecologists), Citizens' Movement, and Radical Socialists (the so-called plural left), won a narrow victory defeating the President's party, the failing government and its beleaguered prime minister. In June, the left formed a government under its leader, Lionel Jospin, and included ministers from all of the formations. Its victory was unexpected as in 1993 the Socialist party had suffered a near obliteration and the conservative right had won a landslide, but it had revived at the 1995 presidential elections, when it ran Lionel Jospin, and steadily—though not spectacularly—revived after that. However, the victory in 1997 was more the result of the conservative right's divisions, an unpopular government, the hostility of the Front National, and the spectacular miscalculations of the neo-Gaullist President Jacques Chirac than to the prowess of the renewed Socialist party.

French Socialist policy was put together initially in the presidential campaign of 1995 with a view to building and maintaining this plural left coalition. Once in power, the government performed competently and was popular, though it was not without its setbacks, and proved administratively effective in the difficult constitutional position of "cohabiting" with the conservative President Chirac. There were problems both with retaining coalition partners and the cohesion of the Cabinet, but the party, under First Secretary François Hollande, proved stolidly supportive of the prime minister. Part of the strategy was to position the premier for the presidential election of 2002 and, when Jospin was eliminated from the runoff, this failed. Jospin's failure was partly personal (a feckless campaign) but was rooted in the contradictions of the Socialist position trying to stretch between the extreme left and the center.

Taking its cue from Mitterrand's dictum that the "party is won from the left," Jospin's strategy in 1995 was to restore the coalition of the left by emphasizing the Socialists' radical and socialist outlook. Its credibility as a governing party was to be restored at the same time, but this came at the price of a continuation of the radical disseverance between "discourse" and practice. Jospin became the Socialists' presidential candidate after a primary against the then First Secretary Henri Emmanuelli in 1995. When he became party leader in the same year, he refashioned it into an instrument for taking power very much through his personal authority. Jospin had no internal opposition to speak of, although there was a "Gauche socialist" faction and the friends of the Speaker (and subsequently finance minister) Laurent Fabius were not the leader's principal claque. Where the left in the 1970s around Chevènement was a serious opponent to Mitterrand's leadership, the Gauche Socialiste was an irritant to Jospin, which, although capable of opposing the leadership on Europe and constantly attacking "neoliberalism," had no alternative to offer. Jospin used his authority to bring the left back to power, but not to revise the party's doctrine or to modernize its appeal on a centrist or "realist" line. Therein lies the distinctiveness of the French party: a government practice that was in line with other European states but an outward hostility to any compromise with socialist ideals and a repudiation of the "Third Way."

Socialist History

In French Socialism there always has been a *décalage* between the radical rhetoric of the party and its timid government practice. Crucially, the French Socialists had to ally with the Communist party (Parti communiste français—PCF) in 1936 and was forced to do so again in the 1970s to build a coalition capable of winning power. Communists polled 28 percent shortly after the Liberation and in the 1960s and 1970s they regularly took more than 20 percent. In addition, the PCF was a massive organization, disciplined, well funded, and with a network of supporting unions, newspapers, and fronts. Hence this alliance reinforced the Socialist party's stance as critic outside the system and alien to its circuits of power. Thus the French never had their "Bad Godesberg" Congress as did the SDP. In the German spa town in 1959, the Social Democrats stripped themselves of the Marxist references from their program to prioritize the humanist tradition of freedom, justice, and solidarity.[1]

This stress on Marx and Marxist purity might explain why the "Bad Godesberg" moment never arrived and why the party had an "opposition" mentality rather than a culture of government. The need to fend off competition from the Communist party and to defend its shaky hold on its own voters, as well as to forge an alliance with them, explains in practical terms why the new Socialists never moved to modernize their party in the 1970s. Socialists defended their positions in the party in the traditional way. All of which meant that there was a vast outpouring of energy, but away from the practical and the pragmatic and into the lyrical and "revolutionary." Eyes were fixed on the far horizons of the revolutionary transformation and not on the quotidian preoccupations of the reformist. In this view, the cathartic moment would be the accession to power of the new team guided by their purity of intentions and morally representing the dispossessed and exploited. They would be able, because they represented the working class and not the "bourgeoisie," to press ahead with necessary policies and they would win. How these were to be effected were of less concern than the need to keep the vision intact.

Thus *Changer la vie*, the party program of 1972, condemned capitalist society for its attendant squalor and inequalities (see 8 and 19). It claimed to be able to "liberate mankind" and end exploitation of man by man. These and other similar references placed it in the long line of socialist documents describing the route to revolution and in that way it was traditional. It was Marxist-based and the vocabulary was certainly Marxist and situated the document in the current of Marxist debate, which at that time pervaded the non-Communist left in France. In the joint Communist/Socialist manifesto of 1972, there was a commitment to the "break with capitalism" and the Marxist influence was reaffirmed.

This socialism was formulaic, but the proposals came from the standard locker of non-Communist solutions, including nationalization and state planning. State industries have a long history in France and one that is not confined to the left (state industry is Royalist in origin), but the assumption was that if the right people (the left) were in charge of the state, industries, and then society, would be changed fundamentally. Under the Socialists, power would move from capital, and from the "multinationals," which were then the object of attack from the left, to the "people" by the agency of the state (14). Planning, through the use of the state's power and through credit, would complete the job of "socializing" the economy, turning it away from production for profit to collective ends. "Nationalization" and "planning," two classic themes, were topped off with a vaguely defined "self-management" ("*autogestion*") that was used to differentiate the Parti Socialiste from the Bolshevism of the Eastern bloc. This would be a new model of society as well as a peaceful revolution of all the classes and groups that were against capitalism, but one that would transform France into a socialist system through a "break" ("*rupture*") with capitalism.

In 1980 the party's *Projet socialiste* came from the same perspective: nationalization of the principal means of production, distribution, and exchange, egalitarianism, the general interest, education and culture, and the alliance of the working class with other "progressive" strata. Its insistence on the "grand soir" remained intact and it also promised to replace capitalism with another type of system ("one not based on profit" [172]) with full employment and a strong growth rate (183). However, it looked to the mechanisms of nationalization, planning, and self-management supported by the "class front" of the exploited and dominated to effect the transformation. It depicted capitalist society, and the "crisis" it was then alleged to be undergoing, in the same lurid terms. It described the "multinationals" grinding down young people and it ascribed to the "rich and powerful" the ambition to subject France to a range of miseries, including the deprivation of liberties and savage repression (370–71). On the other hand, it offered the chance to free humanity and make France the melting pot for the new society (9 and 371).

There was a response to this revolutionary lyricism. Michel Rocard's speech to the party congress in Nantes in 1977 was a veritable hymn to the market economy and a denouncing of the "jacobin, centralizing and state-centered nationalism" (the party program, in so many words). Yet there were strategic reasons (mainly the alliance with the PCF) for emphasizing the "revolutionary line," and Rocard's challenge to the leadership produced a defensive rally around the old ideas that then became a test of loyalty to First Secretary Mitterrand. It became impossible to back down, and even figures like Jacques Delors (famous, in the early 1980s, for being Mrs. Thatcher's favorite finance minister) found it prudent to stay silent or to attack Rocard. All of this ideological posturing took the party further from its modernization away from the "parler vrai" demanded by Rocard and toward the condemnation of the "so-called laws of economics . . . that are nothing more than the principles for running the capitalist system."[2]

First Experience of Government

Opposition mentality persisted and the transformation to a party of government was not even begun by the 1980s, although Rocard's ideas had a bigger audience on the left than was admitted at the time. This period has been summed up as one of triple negation: there was no international crisis (problems were of the French right's making), no problem of competitivity (it was the behavior of the capitalist ruling class that was wrong), and no decline of the working class (only a policy of despoliation). In a stroke of political magic typical of the Houdini that was Mitterrand, the presidential campaigns were always run on a personal platform very different from, and more moderate than, the Socialist party's manifesto.

Unlike the British Labour party, the French Socialists did not have long years of opposition in which to rebuild a realism, and its experience in the 1970s was a contrary one.[3] Parti Socialist reeducation was undertaken on the task and that meant that it was not deep and that it had some peculiar features. But the key change in the double septennate of President Mitterrand was the development of a party of government. In fact, surprisingly, given its long march around the institutions of the Republic, the party adapted quickly to being the support for the government and the president and through a variety of mechanisms became an associate in the Mitterrand system of governance. This enabled the party to profit from the spoils and patronage system typical of French politics of the time and to exploit the funding opportunities suddenly opened to it. In this way, it quickly redefined its role as a party of power and not of opposition and of solidarity with the government, but also, as in some sense, the conscience of the movement and the guarantor of the platform. However, the idea of the party outside parliament laying down the law for the government disappeared and the Socialists accepted the logic of the presidency (though not without some grumblings).

But the experience of government in 1981 was not "lyrical." Even Mitterrand's slimmed-down presidential platform was too radical and impregnated with the "volontariste" ideal of the active state of opposition and not government. Mitterrand confirmed the commitment to the state-centered (jacobin) vision of government and the importance of nationalization in that optic.[4] Three devaluations and a severe balance-of-payments crisis put paid to the dash for growth of the first years. After 1983 the determination to tackle unemployment by reflation waned as this priority gave way to orthodoxy. When it became clear that the direction the government was moving in was not the right one, reservations were expressed (notably by Finance Minister Delors), but not by the party's moderates, who had been silenced. Then there came the Ides of March—the shattering U-turn of March 1983, not unheralded, but all the same a direct contradiction of the message they had promoted in opposition. This U-turn entailed the imposition of austerity measures accompanied by a much more market-oriented policy and priority to the balance of payments. Senior figures in the party were kept informed of the new policy and it was explained to the party executive by the finance minister, but the decision was principally the president's and only very marginally included party figures.[5] Yet the party, controlled by Mitterrand's supporters and pleased to be in power, kept quiet. In large measure the debate was stifled to prevent embarrassing the president and the government, but at the same time the need to retain the Communist party in alliance prevented a real rethink. In 1988 the President's "Lettre aux Français," which served as a manifesto, was virtually free of lyricism and totally free of the apocalyptic language of the past.

One of the key changes was the position of the nationalized industries. French Socialists repudiated any such transformation, and even the term "social democratic" became a hissing and a byword in party debates with most politicians preferring to call themselves "socialists" or perhaps (daringly) "democratic socialists" rather than to align themselves with the northern parties. Sweden was rejected as a model because it had not nationalized industries. It might be noted that the leader of the moderates (Michel Rocard) in the 1970s was condemned for suggesting that the state should take 51 percent stake in industries rather than fully nationalizing them. Nationalization was, then, in French eyes, the test of socialist commitment. In this Socialists also laid claim to the long "jacobin" tradition in French society that emphasized the strong and active state.

It had long been asserted that nationalization was the principal feature of the socialist economy. Hence the greater the extent of nationalization, the more socialist the economy was. But nationalization also had a patriotic and technocratic side developed since the crucial state takeovers at the Liberation under de Gaulle and was the subject of a wide consensus. In 1981 the complete nationalization of six industrial groups, five banks, and state participation in others had created a more extensive state sector than in any other

Western country. Altogether thirteen of the country's largest companies were state owned and state control of industrial turnover was 30 percent. Along with decentralization, this was one of the two principal measures of the septennate and was proof of the socialists' good faith in face of the PCF's criticisms.

The U-turn

The nationalizations in fact proved to be the first step in the liberalization of the economy. New and strong heads were nominated and the companies were rationalized and restructured in preparation for competition on the market (not for a retreat) and their burgeoning deficits were tackled. In 1982 the losses became a major problem and the autonomy of the companies was increased, as was the pace of restructuring. Taking moribund industries, restructuring them and fitting them for the international competition, became under the 1984 government the key "modernization." In French society the idea of nationalization also lost its legitimacy and the left lost one of its elements of identity.[6]

In addition to the idea of "nationalization," the belief of "socialism in one country" had also been dismantled in 1983. Before then, the standard Keynesian remedies were still believed to be valid, but after 1983 they no longer had that status. Thus the Socialist party started by stimulating demand in the economy (chiefly for the less well off) in the hope that this would restart growth. When it produced perverse results, the outlook changed and the emphasis was placed on supply and on competitiveness. They accepted the argument of external constraints and that increasing demand stimulated inflation but that macroeconomic policies did not increase growth and employment.[7] This reduced the differences between left and right and the gap steadily narrowed in subsequent years. By the 1990s the Socialists were also vulnerable on tax and the cost of the welfare state. Bérégovoy, as finance minister and then as prime minister, held to a rigorously orthodox fiscal regime, but the party had deprived itself of the instruments (taxation, price control, state intervention, deficit financing) that differentiated it from the right. No new socialist doctrine appeared to guide the party in an open system, although the left kept up their criticisms of "capitalism."

But the party itself did not debate the U-turn or draw lessons from it. In part this was because the party leadership, the president's supporters, had called on party unity behind the government while they were in power. There were profound disagreements and internal battles, but these were kept behind closed doors.[8] This prudence had the effect of stifling debate in the name of governmental responsibility but also prevented a profound discussion of the U-turn away from the program of the 1970s. It was not possible, so it was asserted, for two lines to exist in the socialist movement: one for the party and one for the government. President Mitterrand in 1984 engaged the new government in a "third way," in between the state power of the past and free-market liberalization. These ideas were wrapped up in the notions of "modernization," enterprise, and efficiency that the Fabius government preached in 1984.

In 1983 this policy was presented as a decision for Europe. It was also a way of putting off the explanation of the reasons for the U-turn and repackaging the market reforms as something else. Spending restraints and return to financial orthodoxy were accepted in these terms (the party was always profoundly pro-European) and accepted by most of the PS—though not by the rest of Chevènement's leftist supporters. This presentation enabled the anti-Europeans to mobilize and find a settled target and has remained a division within the left since that time. Thus an anti-European left emerged mobilized around opposition to Europe—a barn-door target. Voters were able to impute their difficulties and the restrictive economic policies to Europe and the real reason for them was not explained.

When it came to a justification of the U-turn, the party leadership, the other main thought was a "parenthesis." This idea, proposed by the then party leader Lionel Jospin, put off a radical rethink.[9] This idea made the U-turn a matter for the elite who were easily convinced or had probably not believed in the radical program in the first place. However, it was not a cultural conversion of the rank and file. What the "parenthesis" implied was that the party's course was in general sound and that the methods and goals were constant, but also held out was the promise of a return to the policies of 1981. If there had been a temporary lull in the pace of reform, the necessity remained to keep faith with the old values and to avoid absorption of others' principles.[10] Former Prime Minister Mauroy, who had promoted the party's realism while in office, noted, in 1986, the party's determination to "break with capitalism" but added that it was a long-term affair, not one for a single legislative term.[11] From this point of view, the Socialist party had not gone back on its promises and it had remained faithful to them. This became the leitmotif of the party's Bourg-en-Bresse Congress (the first after the U-turn) in the shape of the assertion that fundamentally "nothing had changed." Later it was noted that the policy was to promote reform in other areas to show that the left "remains true to its promises."[12]

This notion of a "parenthesis" and not avowing exactly what the government is doing has been maintained through the 1990s. There were critics, particularly among the partisans of an "alternative politics" based on an even more vigorous state intervention and a dose of protectionism, but the new line was accepted at the party's executive meeting (CD) in March 1983.[13] At that meeting the party leaders were told that it was not realistic to leave the European Monetary System at that juncture and that the government's policy of restraint was a hard choice—though just. Henceforth, it was explained, the necessity would be to reestablish and to "modernize" the economy while maintaining a policy of social solidarity.[14]

But the discussion in the party never took off because the main "modernizers" (Rocard's supporters) decided for internal reasons not to make their own voice too forceful. Rocard did, however, make clear that the implementation of social welfare and other aspirations depended on the vitality of the spirit of enterprise and that the party had yet to accept that.[15] Such views as were expressed from that wing of the party emphasized the need to reform institutions and to open out the state to participation and to make it responsive to the public. Rocard outlined the need to come to terms with a new form of state, not an operator but a facilitator, an organizer of social dialogue and a guardian of the long-term interests of society against the short term of the market.[16]

Theory and Practice

At this point the party's philosophy and mentality again parted company from the practice of the government. Fabius's government restructured the nationalized industries, started the competitive deflation that has characterized economic policy since then, and placed the emphasis on a less engaged state.[17] This view was contrasted with the conservative right (then in Reaganite mode) and its willingness to let the devil take the hindmost. A Socialist government would, by emphasizing education and solidarity, prevent the creation of a laissez-faire market society. However, all the party had to propose were very general statements. There was no new idea to take the place of the Marxism that had once been the dominant mode in its discourse. For most of the late 1980s, the party implemented a form of alliance politics designed to enlarge its support as widely as possible. This was the "catchall" socialist party, but it had no clear substitute for its depassé ideology: nothing replaced nationalization, planning, and self-management. In its limitless pragmatism, it was not all that different from the practice of the old SFIO (with is maximal language and minimal politics).

Rocard, as prime minister in 1988, recognized the problems of the overbearing state and expressed a determination to reform the state and to decentralize it to renovate public services.[18] This went beyond the cosmetic renewal of state property and some staff training and implied a modernization of the state and its contact with people. None of this, it has to be stated, implied a dismantling of the state or a minimal state. At the beginning of the 1990s there was a potential for the clash of ideals, notably between Jean-Pierre Chevènement's supporters, along with Jean Poperen and the modernists around Michel Rocard, who had been joined—in much of their analysis—by some principal Mitterrand supporters. This discussion was also elided in preference to a clash of the factions in 1990 (at the vicious but vacuous Rennes Congress) and then the anodyne final resolution that avoided any issues that might embarrass the government.[19]

A decision was made, however, to define what socialist values were for the next millennium. Chevènement and his group, who believed that the party had sold out, became increasingly dissatisfied and eventually left the party in 1994. It had become an increasingly pragmatic party, and bit by bit the Marxist language of "revolution" and "class struggle" was being stripped out, but the positive sense of direction was missing. President Mitterrand, who traveled ideologically light, saw no point in starting a doctrinal debate as long as the party gave him a free hand (which it did) and undertook no renovation. In 1991 the Congress of the Party at l'Arche completely revised its *projet*, stripped it of its Marxism, and redefined its relation to the market, but this was not much noticed.

It was again Rocard who invited the Socialists to rethink their ideology on the eve of the 1993 elections.[20] In one sense this was apposite. Scandals, failures to cure the malaise of unemployment, and the wearing process of the long Mitterrand presidency had taken their toll on the party and it had to be rebuilt. But it was also in a position of extreme weakness. In the East, the Soviet Union had collapsed and had taken with it the revolutionary future and the idea of the counter model of society. Social democracy had been undermined just at the point where the French party might have been disposed to embrace it. But the party's new policy was never fully "sold" to the activists or the left's voters. As a result, the party's archons were able to pursue policies similar to those on the center right and to make a success of them. However, the education of the party lagged behind and the successes—which were considerable— were hidden by the elite's proclaimed fidelity to traditional socialist values. Hence the party's language was stuck in the groove of the high noon of state intervention of the 1970s. It was the job of presidential candidate Jospin to manage this in 1995 and 1997.

Jospin's Socialist Government

French Socialism remains a "class party" in its own eyes if not in its sociology. It defines itself as the workers' party and talks of alliances between the middle classes and the working and popular classes, even if it no longer sets itself up in an antagonistic opposition to the "bourgeoisie." This is also in part a recognition by the Socialists of their need to come to terms with the middle classes and with the new groups in society reflecting new cleavages in the body politic.

In 1997 Jospin was keen to "say what would be done and do what was said" and avoid the heady rush of a "first hundred days." It was a modest program limited, on the economy, to reducing the workweek, creating 700,000 jobs for the young unemployed, and reorienting the health tax to the CSG. It was, all the same, compared with Blair (who had won in England a few weeks before) and its state direction was contrasted to the New Labour message. Jospin was in agreement with Blair on the outdatedness of the old socialism. But the PS's administrative expertise, the acceptance of the market, regulation, and social security did not serve to differentiate it sufficiently from French conservatives. (Even so, the conservatives helped by criticizing the Socialists' "extremism.")

Jospin's government has been closer in its policies to Rocard's "second left" than to Mitterrand's early jacobin approach. In practice, Jospin went further than the "neither nationalization nor privatization" of 1988, for example, taking up a stance that recalled Rocard's dictum that the state should not be involved in manufacturing but in fact retreating from services and finance as well. Thus, although the state was used to create jobs for the young unemployed, it was not used to take over industries. Jospin noted that "socialism is no longer defined by nationalization" and the government undertook the biggest privatization program in French history.[21] The rapid program of very extensive privatization was set under way touching on the core socialist nationalizations of 1981 and even the Liberation nationalizations. But the Socialist government has refused to refer to "privatizations" (instead calling them "private participation") and has not promoted them as one of its success stories.

Likewise its legislation for the thirty-five-hour workweek, whether or not it created new jobs, introduced a new flexibility. Socialists stated that full employment could not be achieved through a "flexibility" entailing insecurity, but they still noted that this "flexibility" should be negotiated.[22] In the same vein, Labour Minister Aubry's "plan d'aide au retour à l'emploi" was close to Blair's in its thinking, bearing down as it did on fraud to reduce costs and placing the obligation on the unemployed to take work. In 1999 new Finance Minister Fabius even made inroads into the pension system with "épargne salariale" in keeping with Jospin's views.[23] But, unlike Blair and Schröder, the PS is not explicitly inegalitarian.

At the same time, Jospin has sought to improve the responsiveness of the state and to use management tools to promote reforms, but, as the finance minister said, "unlike yesterday's left we must not intervene in the market."[24] Jospin, like Rocard, believes in the active state and the state as the guarantor of equality and opportunity and has been careful to praise public employees (the left polls strongly among public service workers) and tried to keep their support for the proposed reforms. Despite this determination, the public service workers have been reluctant and the extreme left and Chevènement picked up votes on the Socialist's left from the partisans of the jacobin state. In the regional elections of 1998, the European elections of 1999, and the local elections of 2001, this drift from the Socialists was evident. Jospin's view remained that the state should promote innovation and is indeed vital in the modern context. Thus the state has to support and nourish future sources of growth as well as invest in infrastructure and invigorate the business environment.[25] But Jospin was also determined to press ahead with reforms intended to make the state more responsive and accessible.

The Party System

A major constraint is that French Socialism is precariously placed within the party system. Although in 2001 it was the biggest party in France, and it will likely be the principal party of opposition in the future, it depends on its allies. Jospin's government was popular and did withstand the test of power, remarkably holding out against the usual decline in a government's popularity after the second year. However, the Socialist party was not hegemonic on the left as its homologues are in other Western societies. Thus it had the fourth lowest percentage vote of EU socialist parties, and with 58 percent had the lowest share of the total left-wing vote (that is, including the diverse ecologist parties, Communists, etc). It is strong enough to make its will prevail but not strong enough to impose its authority on a fragmented left wing. It has not yet recovered from the ravages of the two Mitterrand septennates and scandals that periodically surface to remind people of that time. It is much more precarious in its hold over the voters than in the 1970s (when it represented a new force), and it is not as popular with the younger generation as it was then.

Socialist party difficulties stem from the nature of the coalition of the "plural left," which it has led since 1997, but this alliance prevents it from moving to the center as Blair has done and as some (the Fabius supporters) in the party propose.[26] Involved in the "plural left" alliance were the Movement of the Radicals of the left, the Verts (the biggest ecology party), the Citizens' Movement, and the Communist party. It was not possible for the Socialists to find a majority in the Assembly without their support, but the real influence of the small partners comes from their ability to attract the voters the Socialists cannot and to put a new face on the Socialist coalition. This alliance of small parties with the Socialists proved less fragile than anticipated (although the minister of the interior resigned) and held together in the face of challenges from the conservative right and the "events" of office for five years. But it was a fissiparous alliance that, by its nature, needs the small parties to assert themselves by criticizing the Socialist party. In the 2002 presidential elections, the left, broadly defined, fielded seven candidates and six of them turned their fire on the Socialist government. Thus there was a tension at its heart that compromised the reelection of the government.

French Socialists still confront the dilemma identified by Przeworski and Sprague in which they have to reach out beyond

their core support to become a majority (catchall) party, but in doing so they lose their traditional working-class support. Socialist
parties, in this view, either cling to their core vote and become marginal to mainstream politics or abandon their ideals and seek middle-
class followers and this way betray their supporters. In the 1980s the
party had a different discourse for each constituency and the presidential election facilitated this simultaneous appeal to moderates
and leftists. In the late 1990s the coalition of the "plural left" performed this function of talking to different constituencies with the
smaller parties picking up support from the voters not amenable to
the Socialist party.

This particular dilemma is acute in the French case because the
main working-class party had until very recently been aligned with
the Communists. Hence the alliance between the Communists and
the Socialists was still the heart of the "plural left," as it was of the
"union of the left" in the 1970s, and the Socialists could not dis-
pense with Communist support if they were to win power at the national level. Unfortunately for the Socialists, the support of other
sectors of opinion is also necessary and alliance with the PCF makes
this difficult—though, evidently, not impossible—and the decline
of the Communists meant that the extreme left had escaped the embrace of the coalition.

French Communism has been in constant and apparently un-
stoppable decline through the Fifth Republic and the alliance with
the Socialist party has not halted that tendency. For the Communist
party, there is a tension between its oppositional tendency developed over the years since its foundation and built to attack the "bour-
geois system" (including the "social democrats") and its need for
alliances. Communism is strong in the unions (CGT is Communist
controlled) and in the run-down industrial and marginal agricultural areas. This is expressed in an anti-Europeanism and fierce an-
ticapitalist rhetoric that, although somewhat attenuated these days,
is still recognizably Marxist. On the other hand, the PCF's remaining strength is in local government, where it has held out against
the trend elsewhere in Europe largely as a result of its organization
and dedication and its alliances with the Socialists. To destroy its
local base would be to reduce the Communist party to the ranks of
the minor left-wing parties on the extreme left. Communist unions
are also strong in nuclear power, which leads to a clash with the
ecologist parties in the alliance. For the Communists the alliance
with the Socialists is a daily struggle between the elements hostile

to "capitalist society" and the reformists who want to collaborate with the PS. The Communist party decline deprived the Socialists of a crucial 5–10 percent and of their powerful electoral and political machine.

But beyond the Communists is the need to retain the left-wing vote. In France the vote for the extreme left in presidential elections and in general and local elections is real and is a manifestation of discontent with the Socialist government. It is the extreme left that has been the beneficiary of Communist decline and not the Socialists or still less the center. Thus the rise of the Trotskyite Lutte Ouvrière and (to a lesser extent) of LCR is a serious treat to the continuation of the coalition and explains why the Socialists have gone out of their way to condemn "neoliberalism" and the new right. They claim to belong to the left but are willing to vote against the "plural left" or to abstain. In the presidential elections of 2002, the Trotskyite candidates polled over 10 percent, and those votes were not additions to the left but appreciably hostile to it.

As much ecologist support as can be garnered is also needed by the Socialist party. In the early 1990s they were well placed to profit from the collapse of the PS, but, disorganized and squabbling, they failed to capitalize on their opportunity. Their divisions and lack of organization counted against them, although they are seen as attractive by most groups in society and have an appeal that goes beyond their limited electoral core. One of the attractions of the ecologist parties was that they had not been pulled into the party system; in becoming part of the government coalition, however, they lose that specificity. Moreover, no real ecologist core had been consolidated in the 1990s and their vote remains highly volatile in what is more naturally an opposition than government movement. Although the Verts (but not all ecologists) are currently on the left, their voters are disinclined to place themselves on the left/right continuum. Ecologists are like the socialists in their antiracism; they promote libertarian values, but they are effective among the young, the middle classes, and those with higher education.

Jean-Pierre Chevènement's small Citizens' Movement was at the outset also a part of the "plural left." This party split from the Socialists in 1994 over the European issue, but it promotes a strong state and has a nationalist policy summed up by the notion of "Republicanism." Its anti-Europeanism sits badly with the PS and the Verts, but not with the PCF, while Chevènement's tough law-and-order policies do not find favor with the ecologists—nor did his crackdown on illegal immigrants. Combining a law-and-order, state interventionist, and anti-European message appeals to important sections on the left and makes a conciliation of the Citizen's Movement. Chevènement played a crucial role as minister of the interior and brought a firmness to policies on crime that did not allow them to be depicted as "soft" on crime. This was a key role in an area of traditional left-wing weakness and where most parties of the left feared to tread. However, in 2000, Chevènement resigned in protest at the government's devolution of power to Corsica and started to campaign for the presidency against the prime minister. This trajectory took Chevènement into calling for the reinforcement of state authority and outside of the left's coalition.

But the Socialists were also faced by competition from the extreme right. Le Pen's Front National appeals to a popular electorate against "them" (the establishment, the "gang of four") through anti-elitist, anti-European, and xenophobic antihumanist messages. Le Pen's has been an attack on the humanitarian and Republican values of the Socialist party; the Front National undermined its support with the working class. Socialists found this attack very difficult to counter given that these values were central to the PS' definition of itself. Le Pen's effect was particularly marked in 1993 (when the PS collapsed) and a "left-wing Lepenism" then appeared, which has continued to take votes from the working class, which might have been expected to vote Socialist. Thus in the 2002 presidential elections, 26.1 percent of workers voted for the Front National, 12 percent for the PS, and only 5.3 percent for the Communists. And those elections made the Front's electorate the most working class with 37 percent to the Socialist's 26 percent and the Communist's 35 percent.[27] Le Pen's Front National was not recognized as a threat. This had two important side effects: (1) it was not the divisive factor on the conservative right that it was, and (2) its formidable reputation as a movement on the march had been undermined and it did not serve as the force to keep the left together in the first ballot of the 2002 presidential elections.

French Socialist difficulties of coalition management are evident at a number of points, but one is an illustration of the problem: the so-called Michelin affair. In September 1999, the head of the Michelin Company rather maladroitly announced that its European organization would be rationalized and that 7,500 jobs would be lost in France. There was consternation, but Jospin, perhaps feeling that this was the time to make a pedagogical point about the new world of global forces and industrial competitiveness, went further than he had gone before. On 13 September he stated that people "should not expect everything from the state and the government." This was too much for the coalition of parties in the "plural left" and an outcry forced the prime minister to back down and to make the traditional response of the left and condemn the company.

Conclusion

In 1997 the Socialist party capitalized on the mistakes of the conservative right and won power for five years. The government had some notable successes (unemployment, in particular, fell noticeably and growth was strong), but they discovered that five years were not enough to effect a real transformation. There were still many unemployed, job security had not been reestablished, and poverty remained widespread with many living on the minimum "dole."[28] Full employment was not restored and the perception of job losses and of increasing employment insecurity was hardly changed.

Politically speaking, Jospin's Socialist government, while denying any capitulation to the marketization vogue, has advanced certain measures as proof of its left-wing credentials. It introduced a thirty-five-hour workweek, extended health and welfare coverage, reduced unemployment by more than a million, and made layoffs of workers more difficult. Probably the most symbolic measure was the thirty-five-hour workweek. On the left the reduction of working hours is a traditional measure (started first by the 1936 Popular Front) and it became the flagship legislation of 1997. It had the good fortune to be opposed by the employers' federation, but it was used to introduce flexibility into working time and in this way to bring down business costs. It was far from being a straightforward attack on market principles or competition, as it was presented, and was opposed by the far left and by some unions.

It was into this context that the debate about the "Third Way" intruded. Blair's determined effort to woo the center and business sector is at cross grains with the French Socialists' need to keep their left-wing support together. Blair and Jospin came to power at the same time (Blair in May and Jospin in June 1997), but their first meeting as Premiers was at the Malmö International Socialist meeting. This was the conference at which Blair invoked the "Third Way" as the future of European Socialism. That necessitated a response from Jospin, who could not accept such a frank, not to say brutal, exposition of the virtues of the free market. An antinomy was set up between the Blair/Schröder vision of flexible labor and capital markets outlined in June 1999 (just before the European elections) and the French party's view.[29]

In a sense, the French Socialist party needed the counterpoint of the Blair/Schröder Third Way to oppose and to enable it to assert its position on the left. In the same way, it needed from time to time the reassuring outrage of the French business community. Thus Jospin chose to stress the need for social solidarity and the respect for national traditions. In addition, the party defended the nation-state and its "framework" for solidarity while claiming to be the most left-wing government in Europe. Blair became something of a bogeyman on the French left and Blair's landslide reelection in June 2001, which came at the same time as the Socialist party's commemoration of its "Epinay Congress" (which defined the party on the "revolutionary left"), was not greeted with rapture; in fact there was some barracking.

In sum, the French Socialist party won the general elections of 1997 because of the mistakes of the conservative right. It proved a competent administrator but did not replace its old doctrine. It has sought to win over the center-floating vote without alienating its core support and was successful enough in 1997 to scrape through with a narrow majority. However, in 2002 it lost on two sides. It went too far to the center (and so lost crucial white-collar and public-sector votes on the left) and the needed support on the left from the Trotskyites and the Chevènementists was not forthcoming. Jospin's Socialists were continually obliged to look to the center and at the same time appeal to the far left. This proved too much: in the presidential elections of 2002, Jospin lost crucial votes on the left to minor candidates (and to Le Pen) and these were not compensated by gains from the center.[30] This is a two-way stretch inherent in the European socialist position, but it is more acute in the French case than in others. With the defeat of Jospin in the 2002 presidential elections, for many years the only figure capable of bringing together both left and center, the party leadership is disputed by personalities preaching a modernizing "Blairite" message that is more likely to split than unite the fragmented left.

Leeds University

Notes

1. W. Paterson and S. Padgett, A History of Social Democracy (London, 1991), 29.

2. As stated by the majority resolution (tabled by Mitterrand and supporters) in the 1979 Metz Socialist Party Congress.

3. A. Bergounioux and G. Grunberg, Le Long Remords du Pouvoir (Paris, 1992).

4. Jean Lacouture, François Mitterrand (Paris, 1998), 1:310.

5. Ibid., 2:283.

6. M. Margainraz, in S. Berstein, ed., François Mitterrand (Paris, 2001).

7. L. Cohen, ed., L'idée socialiste aujourd'hui (Paris, 2001), 41.

8. Jacques Attali, Verbatim (Paris, 1993), 1:414.

9. Lionel Jospin, Un Socialisme du possible (Paris, 1991), 19–20.

10. Lionel Jospin, in Le Monde, 27 August 1983.

11. Revue Politique et Parlementaire, June 1986.

12. T. Pfister, À Matignon au temps de l'union de la gauche (Paris, 1985), 213.

13. W. Northcott, François Mitterrand (London, 1992), 116.

14. J.-L. Bianco in S. Berstein, ed., François Mitterrand (Paris, 2001), and Y. Roucaute, Histoires Socialistes (Paris, 1982).

15. A. Duroy and M. Schneider, Le Roman de la rose (Paris, 1982).

16. Michel Rocard, Un pays comme le notre: Textes politiques, 1986–1989 (Paris, 1989).

17. Cohen, L'idée socialiste aujourd'hui.

18. Rocard, Un pays comme le notre, 100.

19. E. Dupin, Le Disciple (Paris, 1998). L. Jospin, Le socialisme moderne (Paris, 2000).

20. Le Monde, 23 February 1993.

21. Libération, 19 November 1999.

22. Un monde plus juste, 1999 text proposed by the French Socialist Party Executive to the Socialist International conference.

23. Les Echos, 9 December 1997.

24. Libération, 7 June 1998.

25. Lionel Jospin, "Ma sociale-démocratie," Libération, 19 November 1999.

26. Laurent Fabius, Les Chantiers de la gauche moderne (Paris, 2002).

27. Ifop exit poll, in Libération, 22 April 2002.

28. D. Clerc, "Emploi," in Alternatives économiques, no. 201 (March 2002).

29. L. Bonnet et al., Blair-Schröder: Le texte du "manifeste" (Paris, 1999).

30. See D. Collin and J. Cotta, L'Illusion plurielle (Paris, 2001), and G. Desportes and L. Maudit, La gauche imaginaire (Paris, 1999).

UWE JUN

The Changing SPD in the Schröder Era

Public opinion data gathered from the latest surveys on Germany's upcoming parliamentary elections have turned out to be disheartening for the Social Democratic Party (SPD). Without exception, the Social Democrats take second place and lag behind the Christian Democrats (CDU/CSU) by several percentage points (Fig. 1).[1] Today, only a few months before the next parliamentary election, a repetition of the electoral victory to the extent of 1998 seems to be rather unlikely. We are therefore faced with the perplexing question of how the SPD could arrive at such a disadvantageous position given

Fig. 1. The SPD and the CDU at the polls ("Sunday Question")

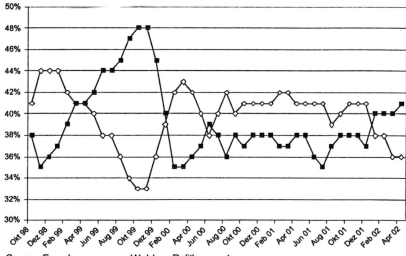

Source: Forschungsgruppe Wahlen: Politbarometer.

I am very grateful to Antje Ellermann (Brandeis University) for giving me helpful comments.

the historic electoral success of 1998, when the party achieved its second-best result at parliamentary elections since Word War II. Is the SPD powerless against a strong tendency of the German electorate to cast its ballot in favor of the CDU/CSU,[2] which has pervaded almost the entire history of the Federal Republic of Germany and has been described as "a permanent discrimination of the SPD against the CDU/CSU in the competition of parties."[3] Or is this situation just a snapshot without deeper consequences for the party?

Have the recent reform efforts on part of the SPD—which undoubtedly contributed to the electoral success of 1998—turned out to be useless or lacking in efficiency? Has the SPD failed to build up a new project of the democratic left? To answer these questions, this essay will investigate, first, the strategies the SPD employed to achieve a majority position in the voter market and, second, how the Social Democrats have been affected by changes in party competition. I will outline recent changes within the SPD and will ask to what extent the party has been able to counter the challenges resulting from the interaction of social, political, and media processes of change. It shows the changes to its communication strategies, the party's internal organization, and, finally, its programmatic agenda. I will argue that the SPD has changed most noticeably in the area of its representation toward the outside world. In particular, it has employed the media as a powerful force. The SPD recognized that professional communication strategies in modern media democracies have become a central factor in gaining and maintaining political power. Politics can present itself primarily by means of successful communication that can be used to develop and mobilize segments of the electorate. Communication in media democracies therefore to a large extent implies communication through the media. This form of communication can capture the attention of the majority of voters and, ultimately, win elections if it does so in ways that are professional, easily noticed, and plain enough to be understood by all electoral groups. I argue that, in order to gain the support of new groups of voters, the SPD has not only changed its communicative forms of presentation but has connected them with a new programmatic orientation. It is important that both communicate the party's future as well as present competency. However, while the SPD was successful in restructuring its communication strategy, this essay will show that the party's programmatic appeal was less convincing. In order to further strengthen the image of a modernized party, the SPD started to resume its organizational reform, begun in 1993, in an attempt to adapt to "modernization requirements."[4] The question to what extent the SPD's processes of change will have repercussions on the German party system as a whole, and what these changes will mean for the future prospects of the SPD, will be the subject of the concluding section.

The SPD's Processes of Change

Changes in Communication Strategy

Because of their organizational structure, political parties today reach a continually declining segment of the electorate via formal channels of their organizations.[5] Social ties have decreased noticeably and the possibilities for political parties to exert influence on their environment by means of personal communication have decreased considerably. Mass media have become the main source of political information for almost all social groups in Western democracies. If mass media choose not to take notice of an issue or event, it has virtually not taken place for the public. As a consequence, the forms of organization-centered party communication (communication within and by the party) have become superseded to a large extent by media-oriented forms of presentation.[6] Political parties use the mass media to present their programmatic agendas and candidates, a process that has gathered speed in the past fifteen to twenty years: "The process of mediatization of political actors, political events, and political discourse is a major trend in political systems of the 1990s."[7] Mass media are offering the necessary public forum for legitimation in the eyes of the voters. To large parties intent on recruiting voters from almost all social groups, they offer the advantage of large reach. This is particularly the case with television as the main medium for political communication.

The struggle for attention in the media meanwhile has become a political necessity for political parties. Because the media have enormously expanded in recent years, they penetrate almost all social sectors of society and continue to absorb an ever-increasing share of the time and attention of the public—the media have become an ever-present fact of life. Without mass media, it is no longer possible to mold public opinion for the simple fact that it is the media that determine public awareness of political actors and their daily actions. Political actors are therefore forced to adopt the logic of the media, and political actors and political processes alike have so to speak become "media-infected."[8] The creation of a political public informed and molded by the media and the improvement of communication competencies by parties have become a central part of politics, especially in the realm of party competition.

Political parties have responded to the most recent challenges of social change (individualization, pluralization of lifestyles, shift of focus in values) and the changes of the media by professionalizing their communication departments, improving their communication performance, and designing modern communication strategies. This response is to be understood as a necessity for parties both to become and remain powerful political forces in a highly complex and differentiated media world: "Modern parties have been forced to adapt, with greater or lesser success, to the new communications environment if they are to survive unscathed."[9] For this purpose, political parties increasingly engage the services of external PR consultants, marketing specialists, and other experts of persuasive communication.

The SPD has not ignored this general development of political parties. On the contrary, professionalization and personalization, the application of the latest media-suited methods of mass communication, have become an integral part of the SPD since the election campaign of 1998.[10] The 1998 election campaign shall be considered as the starting point of the SPD's communication modernization and I will briefly discuss it here.

With its KAMPA election campaign center, the SPD in 1998 established a service center outside the party headquarters that closely cooperated with professional specialists from the areas of advertising, marketing, multimedia, event organization, and public-opinion polling.[11] Crucially, these forms of cooperation with professional agencies and public-opinion poll institutes continued even after the election campaign in order to ensure the expansion of effective and modern management and communication structures within the SPD. To party secretary (Bundesgeschäftsführer) Machnig, this direction of future party activities, which was increasingly pursued in the second half of the 1990s, is no longer reversible. In the future, logically consistent forms of media presentation shall be given at least the same priority as programmatic work. This is a bold proposal for a party that has conceived of itself for more than one hundred years as an essentially programmatic party. Medium to long-term campaign planning, expansion of the professionalization of the organization, campaign forms and communication lines, personalization as a strategic element of positive image creation, and a strengthening of Federal Chancellor Schröder, an increased use of symbols for the dissemination of ideas and values—these are all central elements of the SPD's communication strategy.[12] The coverage of issues perceived as deciding factors in elections can be added to this. To the SPD, this means to demonstrate competency in those areas of politics, and mainly with regard to those issues that are at the top of the agenda in media reporting. But also to be the subject of media reporting and not only its object, it is necessary for the SPD to try and concentrate communication and external presentation of content on "winner issues."[13] To achieve this, the party also relies on emotion, simplification, symbols, and state-of-the-art visual forms of presentation as well as marketing and advertising rules. In Machnig's words: "Political communication has to take into account the aesthetic rules of the media if it wants to achieve the goal of conveying security, reliability, and hope."[14] According to Machnig, it is necessary that the advertising measures of parties should match the standards of commercial advertising.

A clear image uniformity of presentation and a unified message—all present in the election campaign 1998—appear to be important prerequisites for the successful implementation of communication strategies. However, what proved decisive was the fact that in the SPD's presidium, principal issues and operational decisions were coordinated and directed with the extraparliamentary party, the parliamentary group, and state governments.[15] This strengthening of the party leadership in the political process follows research findings that party leaders should, in order to adapt successfully to dynamically changing framework conditions, dispose of a relatively high degree of autonomy in order to be able to make strategic adaptations to changes in the voter market. This implies that especially in large parties the relevant leadership is more voter-oriented than other party segments such as activists and individual members. If political parties such as the SPD are regarded as "loosely coupled anarchies"[16] characterized by organizational variety and a relatively large amount of autonomy of individual organizational parts, their actions quite frequently run counter to systematic or efficient action. On the contrary, top-down models of party organization seem to be more suited to develop and ensure adequate strategies for parties to succeed against their competitors in media democracies. But since these do not satisfy the organizational variety of large modern parties, a greater degree of autonomy for party leaders in strategic and programmatic issues seems to offer a way out to produce organizational efficiency without negating participation claims that are mainly asserted at lower party levels. The introduction of intraparty plebiscitary elements can fulfill this function at the federal level. The party model, described by Machnig as a "network party" (*Netzwerkpartei*),[17] is by no means hesitant to respond to claims for more participation, thereby approaching the notion of political parties as "centralized election campaign organizations"[18] or "professionalized voter parties." Machnig makes his argument by placing professionalization in the forefront and simultaneously combining party leadership loosely with networks that are effective in the social sphere. The term that seems most appropriate here is "professionalized media communication party." In each of these models, party leadership disposes of comparably large maneuvering space in the conception of strategies.

However, to permanently secure these structures it is insufficient to implement them in an ad hoc and informal manner; they have to be permanently anchored in the organization by means of reforms. Accordingly, first steps were initiated by SPD secretary-general Müntefering by intraparty reforms under the slogan "democracy needs party."

Changes in Organizational Structure

The organizational reforms designed by Franz Müntefering under the title "democracy needs party"[19] consisted of a number of crucial elements. The concept of Social Democratic organizational reform dates back to the modernization of party structures under party chairman Björn Engholm in 1993 that were discussed under the label "SPD 2000."[20] There the primary task was to counter the emerging erosion of the SPD as a member party through greater inclusion of nonmembers in party work and more decision rights for members. The latter, however, just like the introduction of direct-democratic elements such as primary elections, member interviews, and member decisions, do not feature prominently in the "democracy needs party" program; they merely feature in the proposal to introduce preliminary elections for federal parliamentary candidates. To Müntefering, the opening of the party for nonmembers, the qualification of full-time members and mandate holders of the party, and the strengthening of the SPD's external presentation by increased communication and dialogue competency is of primary importance. Thus it is important to pay close attention to both the need to strengthen the ability of the SPD to act as a socially relevant organization and to adapt it to the requirements of the media society.[21]

Opening of Party Structures: The Müntefering plan calls for a "dialogue with interested parties, also with those outside the party" and proposes to take advantage of the political potential of those "who do not want to work in fixed structures."[22] More concretely, these aims find expression in proposals to reserve promising spots on the regional candidate lists for the federal parliamentary election in 2002 for presently inactive party members. This in effect eases the leap into professional politics for persons entering through the back door. In accordance with this, beginning with the federal parliamentary elections of 2006, even preliminary elections for the nomination of candidates are to be open to all persons from a constituency entitled to vote. Hitherto passive members shall also be increasingly included in party work by an extension of offers for participation, without, however, defining this aspect more precisely. This process of "flexibilization" of organizational structures shall apply to all levels of party work from the local to the federal level.

Qualification of Mandate Holders and Full-Time Staff: To the SPD, the qualification of party representatives, staff, and functionaries on an honorary basis to tackle changing political challenges is one of the main tasks of future organizational work. All full-time party staff will be "prepared for their new tasks as moderators and communicators,"[23] which mainly means to improve their presentation techniques and forms in the media. The same applies to numerous representatives of the party in parliaments and governments. The party plans to establish a "municipal academy" to train young political talents for leadership posts at the municipal level. Efforts to increase its recruiting competency will include qualification measures at various levels by means of a "professionalization of intra-party educational work."[24] Finally, to underline the goal of promoting young talents in the future SPD's parliamentary group, the party aims at including thirty members younger than forty ("30 out of 40").

Strengthening of Communication Competency: According to Machnig, party communication has to be modernized and professionalized. With regard to external party communication, this means that the SPD assert itself in the contested market for media attention. For internal party communication, the Internet shall increasingly be used as a means of information dissemination and exchange. Under the catchword "digital party," the SPD subsumes a faster and direct form of internal communication by an intranet installed for this purpose by means of which the party headquarters are connected with divisions at the state, district, and county level and into which local party organizations will be integrated. Thereby an intraparty communication system will be set up that offers horizontal and vertical connection channels and interfaces and provides for permeability. But so far this system is hardly usable; it functions more as a top-down instrument of information transmission of the full-time staff and management area controlled by the party leadership.

In addition to improving its media communication competency, the SPD also strives to create avenues of direct communication. It does so by building up contacts with "politically interested citizens who are not bound to a particular party" and cannot be reached via "classical party structures,"[25] thereby connecting forms of direct communication with media communication. Nevertheless, it clearly gives precedence to the latter because, in contrast to concrete ideas in the media communication area, there are no precise proposals on how to organize the democratic discourse of party members in a more functional manner. The structural opening toward nonmembers and the increased inclusion of more passive members clearly reflect a trend toward professionalized and commercialized party activism in which the long-standing trend toward a declining significance of party membership is further intensified.[26]

Once again we can observe a lack of certainty in Müntefering's proposals: while he does not principally question the organizational structure of the member party, many of his proposals point to turning away from it, such as the introduction of preliminary elections, the increased inclusion of nonmembers in party activities, or the intensified turning to professional media communication, which, because of its structural preference for party leadership and external consultants, also serves to reduce opportunities for members to participate. As was the case at the time, once direct democratic elements with increased participation opportunities for individual members were introduced, the groups of middle and lower-level functionaries, the activists, would lose influence over decision-making processes.[27] In view of this media orientation, the member organization has become almost meaningless as an election campaign resource.[28] If leadership deprives active members of their exclusive participation rights, such as program development or nomination of candidates, it can consequently also move away from the model of the member party. Already in 1994, Leif and Raschke stated that the democratic member party is worn down in the contradiction between participational revolution and mass-media deformation.[29] As the old functionary party starts increasingly to dissolve, the organizational structure of the member party sees itself more and more being called into question.[30]

Müntefering's proposals were heatedly discussed within the SPD, in particular the question of whether this tendency was going to continue. Debates were most intense in the preeminent state of the old established functionaries of Social Democrats, North Rhine-Westphalia, where Müntefering as state chairman had instigated principal structural reforms and, through the dissolution of former district organizations, had asserted himself against the protectors of traditional structures. Especially Müntefering's proposal regarding preliminary elections for federal parliamentary candidates encountered great skepticism in the federal party and was rejected by the party chairmanship.

Programmatic and Policy Changes

Within the SPD, Giddens's idea of the "Third Way" has had a much smaller impact on the programmatic discussion than in the British Labour party. It was not until the publication of the so-called Schröder-Blair Paper,[31] in the spring of 1999, that a public discussion on the Third Way got under way. However, this discussion disappeared relatively soon after it had arrived at the forefront of public debate. Since then, the programmatic discourse of the SPD has been held almost exclusively within the party, without attracting much media attention. Although the party conference in Berlin in 1999 called for a commission to draw up a new basic program, which since then has discussed its ideas and proposals with employers, interest organizations, nongovernmental organizations, scientists, and international partner organizations, the public has taken no notice of its work. By taking this "courageous step"[32] of drawing up a new basic program, the SPD has tried to counter the often-heard criticism that the party exists in a programmatic vacuum.[33] The still effective basic program, the Berlin Program from 1989 (Berliner Programm), is in the eyes of its critics no longer in keeping with the times, is incoherent and, from the moment of its adoption, has been outdated, thereby being unable to serve as a compass for politics in the united Germany.[34] The Berlin Program is an attempt to reconcile the old and the new left. It combines the traditional social democratic values of the labor movement with the ecological and postmaterialist values of left-libertarian movements that have arisen from the student protests of the late 1960s and have incorporated new ideas concerning the role of the welfare state in an era of globalization. However, this mixture failed to improve the position of the SPD in the electoral market. Political scientists seem to concur that the conclusion of the Berlin Program was "robbed of all impact."[35] As Keynesian ideas were abandoned, so was the traditional aim of economic growth and the program failed to fill the void with a new consistent concept of social and economic policy. The SPD remained in a position between modernization and tradition.

Since the early 1990s, the modernization process has evolved slowly and incrementally. The Berlin Program did not play any important role in this process. For example, the phrase "Democratic Socialism," a key principle of the Berlin Program, has rarely been mentioned since the early 1990s and has been neglected since Schröder became chairman of the party. In the election programs of 1994 and 1998, as well as in the recent report of the program commission, the phrase was not even used. Economic and social issues were at the core of both election campaigns, in particular in 1998. Economic modernization and social justice (*Innovation und Gerechtigkeit*) were the main themes of the SPD in 1994 and 1998; the ecological impetus of the Berlin Program with its skeptical implications concerning economic growth and modern technology was taking a back seat. With the resignation of Lafontaine as party chairman, the modernizers and the supporters of the "New Politics group"[36] with their pragmatic attitude and stance were prevailing over the left.[37] These groups are more unequivocally oriented toward gaining and maintaining power than all other factions within the SPD. From their perspective, the parliamentary election in 1998 was an indication that they had chosen the better strategy because the party won votes from highly divergent segments of the electorate without losing votes from its electoral base.[38]

While the program commission of the SPD still meets to develop its new program on general principles under the executive direction of the deputy party chairman Rudolf Scharping, future SPD policy directions are reflected in the party's current discussion paper and its recent government policy.[39]

As the party of the *Neue Mitte*, the SPD as a party in government has taken on new ideas arising from Anthony Giddens's *Third*

Way, without systematically integrating them in a coherent structure, neither in its programmatic concepts nor in its government policy. Classic social democratic topics such as traditional labor policy, a reform of codetermination structures between employers and employees in favor of trade unions, more protection against unlawful dismissal, legal claims to part-time working arrangements, and an extension of jobs that require contributions to the different social insurance funds (health, pensions, unemployment) are added to this. For instance, a change in law increased the payment of replacement wages in cases of sickness to one hundred percent. It is in this context that Schabedoth concludes that SPD policy is an attempt to define traditional social democratic and trade-union policies as an object of interest to the core electorate, thereby bolstering the party's electoral base.[40]

What are the main aspects of the SPD/Greens government policy? First of all, the policy of the SPD/Greens government coalition is different from that of New Labour because of its sustained adherence to the universalistic welfare state. The aim of the SPD is to hold on to the fundamentals of the present social insurance; reforms within the system should stabilize, not restrain it. The introduction of a state-subsidized private capital investment pension as a supplement to the public pension symbolizes such a system change within the boundaries of the universalistic welfare state. Because the SPD continues to conceive of social security as a basic social right, the social insurance system has to ensure economic security and the government has to balance and regulate the market for guaranteeing social security to all individuals. An active government, coupled with strong public institutions and a well-developed welfare state, therefore has to preserve the basic values of the left such as solidarity and equality.

A transition to an activating social investment state has been carried out only partly by the SPD. Pension reform with its strengthening of self-provision after retiring from the labor market is one part of the aspired encouragement of individual initiative; the SPD demands that individuals assume responsibility for themselves and their economic security. It is the role of the activating social investment state to support individuals to acquire knowledge and competence in order for them to make use of income opportunities in a self-reliant and socially integrated manner. Primarily, justice means access for all and equality of opportunity. The emphasis is on a new distribution of opportunities, not on equality of outcome. Accordingly, everyone shall have the same access to education, work, and information; participation in society is possible only on this basis and its implementation depends upon the guarantee of social rights and equality of opportunity. To secure participation is regarded as crucial for a forward-looking social policy. Nevertheless, the system of social security as a form of compensation for income and individual support has remained almost completely unchanged; it has only been supplemented with effective incentives to take a job or to receive guidance from the Employment Office.

It is the task of the welfare state to ensure access to second opportunities, to be understood as "help for self-help." But the SPD's proposal does not go as far as Giddens's proposal to construct a concept of positive welfare in which inefficient and too protective practices of the welfare state are abandoned and replaced by investments in human capital (education and training). While in Giddens's "Third Way" the individual loses the right to adequate social security benefits if he or she fails to seize existing opportunities—it is the task of the state to ensure investment in human capital, rather than security—the protective character of the state remains distinct in SPD policy. Giddens's guiding star of individual responsibility and flexibility can also be found in the government policy of the SPD and Greens, but it has not been pushed to the center of the various reform initiatives. Following this, the expansion of education as a main project of future government policy has not been pursued with much fervor by the SPD. According to Giddens, the state should support individual willingness for lifelong learning so that it will become a matter of course to continue to learn and to gain qualifications in the future. It follows that research and education should be promoted more vigorously. Even though all elements of public and individual investment appear in the SPD's program, recognized by Wolfgang Merkel as the cornerstones of the Giddens model (education, lifelong learning, and the creation of a far-reaching equality of opportunity),[41] they are not equally valued.

For example, the mixture of protection and activation in the SPD's policy can be seen in the *Kombilohn-Model* ("combined earnings model") or "Jump," a program designed for unemployed youth. This program provides for state-subsidized jobs for young people under the age of twenty-five who have been unemployed for more than three months or are poorly qualified. Instead of taking a subsidized job, they can participate in education programs to improve their skills. A reduction or even a deep cut in social security benefits in the event that the unemployed refuses both options, as has been the case in Britain, was not implemented in Germany to any significant degree. The *Kombilohn-Model* was introduced at the beginning of 2002: unemployed persons and recipients of social assistance (*Sozialhilfeempfänger*) receive a subsidy to their social insurance contributions and higher family allowances for a maximum of three years if they take a low-wage job. With the so-called *Job-Aqtiv-Gesetz* ("active job law"), the state pays allowances for the employment of former unemployed persons in temporarily vacant positions, qualification programs for less qualified or older employees, people in irregular employment, and single parents who are taking part in qualification programs. A reduction of social security benefits is in store for all these groups if they reject the various job offers, though this is rarely implemented. The SPD application devotes little space to determining the new relation of state and civil society, a relationship that Giddens considers central. In the recent report of the program commission, a political division of labor between the state and civil society is proclaimed without, however, assuming concrete form. Merely one supplementation of the social state and its instruments by civil commitment is mentioned: voluntary work shall be revalued. Democratization of society with a transparent and more open organization of the public sector and efficient administration and the role of the state as risk-manager are not mentioned. Under the plan of its secretary-general Müntefering, the SPD nevertheless advocates a stronger emphasis on forms of direct democracy, such as petitions for plebiscites and referendums or the right to put forward legal initiatives. It also calls for a strengthening of the family as the basis of societal life and deems the equality of the sexes as important as financial incentives for raising children. The program commission calls for the introduction of all-day child-care facilities in all areas of the country to find better ways to combine parenthood and employment.

In the future, it is envisaged that the SPD's policy be characterized by a so-called "lasting national strategy" that will comprise all social and political areas. Policy will be designed for the long term, in particular budgetary, environmental, and consumer protection policy, and will be informed by long-term considerations.

Another main strategy of the SPD/Greens coalition government's policy can be observed in the establishment of consensus meetings to create a result-oriented culture of dialogue among politics, science, the economy, and the public.[42] These reform- and result-oriented meetings, mostly initiated by the government, are intended to neutralize ideological divergence, bring closer together the different interests through a bargaining process, and generate consensus-oriented solutions in different policy areas. Norms, principles, problems, and procedures of this process are to be balanced between the different actors in order to achieve mutual accordance and cooperation. At the end of the process are joint solutions and the potential for action. In this process, the government primarily assumes the part of a moderator that gives social actors their public space through making available to them its organizational resources.

The best-known and most important forum is the so-called *Bündnis für Arbeit* (Alliance for Employment), which forges trilateral agreements among federal government, employers, and employees in the areas of wage determination, labor market and economic policy, and codetermination of workers. From the government's perspective, the forum's overall goal is to increase the competitive capacity of Germany in the context of globalization by simultaneously increasing economic efficiency and employment.[43] Priority is attached to paid work: it shall function as the basis for organizing one's life and open up opportunities in life. The government saw these trilateral discussions as an efficient way to pass resolutions, to reduce mass unemployment, and to increase flexibility in the labor market. But conflicting strategies and a polarized atmosphere between employers and trade unions revealed the limitations of this corporatist strategy. While other forums such as the one on immigration, the ethics commission, or the initiative for exiting nuclear energy can be evaluated as rather successful, the results from the *Bündnis für Arbeit* are modest indeed: neither could structural unemployment be reduced substantially nor has the flexibility of the labor market been increased. Social and economic policy inertia on both sides—trade unions and employers—is responsible for this result. The capacity of the government turned out to be insufficient. The obstructions, which are partly set up by the German political system with its various veto players, were too high to overcome.

Other policy provisions and instruments for achieving economic efficiency showed varying degrees of success: budget discipline and consolidation at the national level has been contrasted with additional expenditure on the part of the federal states (*Länder*) and local communities (*Gemeinden*). Tax reductions for enterprises and employees have been partly neutralized by increases in indirect taxes (in particular for energy and oil products with the ecological tax reform), while the limitation of the social security system (especially pensions and health) has been counterbalanced by demographic developments. Since 2001, an economic recession has led to a deterioration of the labor market. The successes of the Schröder administration thus are limited. To some extent this result can be explained by the lack of coherence of SPD policy: in its government policy as well as in its programmatic drafts, various assessments and tendencies have not been transformed into a conclusive comprehensive concept. Three closely connected reasons are responsible for this shortcoming:

1. *Insufficient preparation of policy contents and programmatic appeal as a party in government.* The "pragmatic policy reforms"[44] could not refer to any coherent programmatic reform made during the years in opposition. This was prevented by personnel turnover and reformatory efforts that were too ambitious. A not insignificant number of drafts, which had been compiled as an opposition party, were not sufficient or not realizable because of administrative difficulties or inaccuracies with regard to its contents. The often-changing chairmen of the party during the nineties (Engholm, Scharping, Lafontaine, Schröder) were either in charge for periods of time too short to successfully implement fundamental programmatic changes or had no deeper interest in programmatic development. One of the reasons for this attitude can be attributed to the need to overcome inner-party opposition, an undertaking that can stretch over long periods of time. Inner-party consolidation stood in the foreground of the actions of the different party chairmen. Another reason underlying this behavior is the relatively strong position of the SPD in the second chamber of parliament (*Bundesrat*), which gave the SPD opportunities to contribute to shaping policy, so that the use of power instruments or the solution of everyday problems in politics overlapped with the discussion of programmatic basic questions.

2. *Prevailing pragmatism of government policy because of electoral and strategic imperatives.* To gain the support of a majority of voters, the SPD is dependent on highly differentiated voter groups, a fact that has motivated Chancellor Schröder and his consultants to consider carefully the results from qualitative and quantitative opinion research. The SPD's preferred style of governing, "leadership and consensus" (*Führung und Konsens*, Steinmeier 2001), shows that the profile of the SPD

as governing party is less oriented toward coherent programmatic principles than toward credible and majority-producing projects and issues that are able to determine the political
and media agenda, win the votes of these different groups,
and promise better opportunity. Applicability, not programmatic principles, determines the policy of the Schröder administration. The enforcement of majority-producing issues
means not claiming an opinion-leading position, but rather
standing on the top of the majority opinion with arguments,
guided by only some key principles, in order to obtain the
support of these groups. In the SPD the prevailing view considers that in media democracies basic programs or coherent
policy concepts have no significant impact on voters. Key values, images, and the assignment of competence to a party in
policy areas are considered more important.

3. *Heterogeneity of members and voters.* Because of its heterogeneous organizational structure, which became even more so
after the dissolution of formerly powerful groups and factions
in the 1990s, the party leadership was more occupied with
inner-party consolidation than with sharpening a programmatic profile. During the election campaign in 1998, the SPD
succeeded in bringing together these heterogeneous voter
groups and various milieus with leaders—Lafontaine as party
chairman and Schröder as chancellor—with different policy
ideas, without reaching an agreement about future concepts.
Although Schröder was successful against Lafontaine after-
ward and Lafontaine resigned early after the election (with
the consequence that the left wing of the party became almost marginalized), heterogeneity still characterizes the SPD.
Schröder had to take into consideration the attitudes, opin-
ions, and interests of the various groups within the party and
its different voters, not only for strategic and tactical reasons
but also in order to strengthen his own position as party leader.
As a result, the modernizer Schröder was at the same time
the protector of the welfare state. Pragmatism seemed to be
the solution to these sometimes antagonistic expectations that
Schröder had to reconcile. At the beginning of the election
campaign of 2002, Schröder clearly dominates his party,
though "leadership and consensus" seems to be his motto as
party chairman, too. However, this applies more to his efforts to
reconcile different policy positions than to his leadership style.

Fig. 2. Satisfaction with the performance of government and opposition

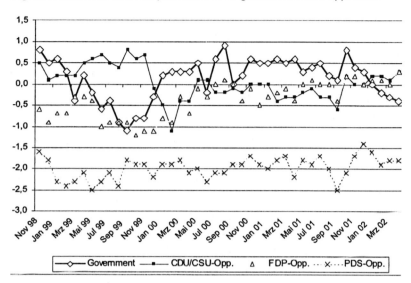

Source: Forschungsgruppe Wahlen: Politbarometer.

To sum up: the SPD still prefers the traditional universalistic, corporatist-statist welfare state without developing fundamental innovations. The party aims at promoting self-responsibility and social inclusion, though it has had no substantial achievements so far. A reduction of state regulation is also hardly noticeable and the German welfare state still shows a high degree of jobless growth. We are left to ponder the question of what social and economic actors will be able to increase employment in the future? In the public sector, the number of persons employed can hardly be increased further. An activating labor market policy and experiments with subsidized low-wage areas are to be understood as merely supplementing measures. In accordance with the conception of the "Third Way," government policy has the tendency primarily to reduce the role of the state to take on tasks neglected by the market, such as the creation of infrastructure measures and the promotion of education and training. However, under the special conditions of Germany's federal system, both are enforceable only with the cooperation of the executives of the federal states.

Different approaches and tendencies are still noticeable in the government's program, though a clearly coherent orientation of its policy can be identified only rudimentarily. As a result, there is growing dissatisfaction in the electorate with the performance of the government (see Fig. 2).

It is clear that the coalition government does not intend a lasting dismantling of the welfare state and that the SPD has taken the path of the moderate consensual welfare state.[45] Even though it aims for autonomy and participation, the coalition government has not yet made any major progress. The planned pension reform, with a strengthening of individual provision for old age after retirement, and the already established tax reform can, nevertheless, be cited as two examples that show the coalition government is not only prepared to carry out drastic reforms but also to enforce them in the face of political opposition.

The Changed Position of the SPD in the German Party System

After discussing changes in communication strategy, the reforms of the party's organizational structure, and programmatic changes, I shall now briefly analyze the altered position of the SPD in the competition of parties. The changing position of the SPD in the party system is not only determined by the party itself but is the consequence of several factors, including the changes within other relevant parties and changing interactions between the individual parties. These in turn are codetermined by general and political developments. I will concentrate only on factors that directly concern the SPD and not on the recent overall development of the German party system.

Electoral Gains of 1998 and Its Consequences

In 1998, the SPD for the second time became the strongest party in the history of the Federal Republic in federal parliamentary elections. With a proportion of 40.9 percent of second votes, it was 5.8 percentage points ahead of the CDU, which is so far the SPD's greatest lead in elections to the *Bundestag*. The desire for a change of government and the CDU's loss in competency in election-deciding political areas, especially in East Germany,[46] were reasons for this development, just like the favorable positioning of the SPD on key issues, the popularity of its chancellor candidate, and the successful election campaign. The election campaign of the SPD in 1998 can be seen as extraordinarily successful, whereby special mention has to be made of its differentiated target-group appeal tailored to individual groups of voters and the imaginative spots and slogans with which it was possible simultaneously to address vastly divergent groups of voters. In particular, "the election was won in the center-oriented, middle-aged middle class in the west, and manual workers in the east, groups of weakly attached voters whose loyalties to the SPD can be expected to be shallow."[47]

The SPD thereby simultaneously owes its success to its image as *Partei der neuen Mitte*, with which it was able to bring on board decisive nonaligned voter groups from the new middle classes, and to its image as the "social justice" party, whereby it managed to mobilize its own loyal voters. In 1998, groups organized in trade unions voted to a great extent for the SPD. For the first time since the Schmidt era, the SPD also won back again the rarely party-aligned voters of the lower middle classes to the detriment of the CDU. The strategy of the "SPD of the modern center" proved to be a success for the party insofar as it managed to integrate extremely different groups of voters. Nevertheless, this heterogeneity of its electorate is at the same time a structural problem for the SPD. As a governing party, it has to make policies that take into account different needs and comply with the interests of extremely disparate groups of voters if in the medium term it does not want to lose its majority position to the Christian Democrats. To achieve its goals, the SPD must gain the support of a host of diverse social groups, ranging from blue-collar workers to salaried professionals.[48] The SPD strategists have to keep in mind that the center-left victory of 1998 seems to be the result of situational factors, far from signifying a structural realignment.[49]

Linking different groups of voters into a majority coalition was accomplished in the parliamentary elections of 1998 by means of symbolic contents and personnel: Schröder, candidate for chancellor, and the then party chairman Lafontaine represented different groups of voters and different political platforms that were united by the SPD slogan "Innovation and Justice." As the central figure of the election campaign, Schröder stood for innovation, with his economic competency and future orientation, and thus was perceived by voters to be more modern in outlook than the incumbent Kohl. Lafontaine, on the other hand, appearing as number two, embodied the social conscience of his party.

In the meantime, the SPD has also developed structures that meet the requirements of daily government routines together with a more efficient control center of government work: representatives of the chancellery, extra-parliamentary party, parliamentary party group, and important state governments now come together for regular informal meetings. In addition, the center of the so-called "situation briefings" of the party in the chancellery is formed by the chancellor and the undersecretary in the chancellery and long-standing Schröder confidant Steinmeier, chairman of the parliamentary party group Struck, and SPD secretary-general Müntefering. Communication with the chancelleries of the state governments headed by the SPD always takes place on Mondays before the meetings of the executive committee and party executive.

It is to the SPD's benefit that the CDU and CSU so far have not developed a coherent opposition strategy. Their opposition rather tends to the competitive side[50] but in the eyes of many lacks clearly distinguishable alternatives to the government's policies. Others see the Schröder administration's willingness to compromise as more obstructive than constructive.

Coalitions and Perspectives on the German Party System

The coalition government of SPD and Greens is the first in the history of the Federal Republic in which both coalition partners moved directly from opposition into government. Even though the formation of the red-green coalition government was also the one that was most likely among all possible coalition variants, the leadership of the Social Democrats had kept open the coalition question before the election and had also taken into consideration other options, such as a grand coalition with the Christian Democrats or the formation of a government with the Liberals (FDP). Only a coalition with the Socialists (PDS) was precluded. But a majority within the SPD then clearly advocated the formation of a coalition with the Greens, to whom they were relatively close programmatically in spite of some normative differences in the eco-libertarian area,[51] especially in the market-justice dimension (Fig. 3).[52]

The pragmatic attitude of the Greens during the coalition negotiations, the joint opposition experience of both parties, and the dominant position of the *real*-political wing in the parliamentary party group of the Greens had a positive impact on the SPD during the coalition-building process.

The fact that the SPD has various coalition options and also exercises them in the federal states (at the state level, it governs with the CDU, just as it does with the FDP, PDS, and Greens) can

Fig. 3. Structure of the German party system (value orientations of party supporters and members)

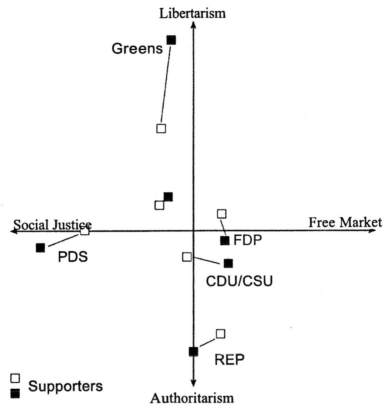

Source: Raschke 2001.

be attributed to its strategically central position within the structure of the German party system. In comparison with all other relevant parties, it is the only one able to enter into various coalitions.
Regarding the PDS, the SPD now as before distances itself at the
federal level; meanwhile, the PDS still has not clearly defined its
coalition policy. All other relevant parties are clearly more restricted
than the Social Democrats in coalition options. Thus the SPD has
profited most from the changes of the West German party system
after the completion of political unification insofar that it has moved
into a core position from which it can easily reach parliamentary
majorities. The other parties of the left, the PDS and Greens, are its
exclusive coalition potential since both parties have ruled out a

coalition with the Christian Democrats, and vice versa. The center-right, the CDU and FDP, is thereby at a disadvantage in the competition of parties because it is dependent on its own majorities or has to consider the SPD as its coalition partner. In the medium term, no fundamental change in this constellation is expected. Because of the present structure of the German party system, it may be anticipated that in spite of the convergence of the FDP and SPD, both in terms of symbolic message and contents (which incidentally also finds expression in changes in party chairman from Lafontaine to Schröder and Gerhard to Westerwelle), the SPD aims at a continuation of the present coalition government. In the end, the Greens are not only closer to the SPD with regard to content, but, according to Raschke's research results, suffer from structural weaknesses in their ability to assert themselves vis-à-vis the larger coalition partner. All of this may have prompted Chancellor Schröder to take the surprising step of announcing in public at a relatively early stage that a continuation of the coalition with the Greens is likely after the coming election.

The East German Federal States and the
Overall Development of the SPD

In comparison with the West German *Länder*, the SPD in the East German federal states is anything but a large party with many members. Karsten Grabow characterizes the organizations of the East German state parties of the CDU and SPD as "election-professionalized framework associations"[53] whereby the SPD lacks the character of a people's party (*Volkspartei*) to a greater extent than does the CDU. With about 27,000 members, the SPD does not have a mass basis in the new federal states and is to a great extent represented and dominated by a small number of outstanding personalities in the executive and legislature.[54] Also at the voter level, the SPD's profile in East Germany is different compared to that in West Germany: in the parliamentary election in East Germany, the SPD for the first time gained a majority among the traditional workforce. At the same time, in the socially balanced structure of the electorate,[55] the social democratic mainstream and the social democratic intelligence classes dominate, while social democratic postmaterialism groups are absent, and the SPD is losing potential voters to the social democratic populism of the PDS. Factors that after the fall of the Berlin Wall were initially assumed to benefit the SPD, such as the "definitely more left"[56] political culture of East Germany, the large number of people who do not subscribe to religion, and the small number of Catholics, turned out to be false. This is because the SPD has a strong competitor on the left of the party, the PDS, and the rather weak party alignment in the East. Traditional party loyalties are present only to a small degree in the East German federal states. All this results in a lower number of loyal voters for the SPD in a regional three-party system, in which, according to Kießling, the main conflict runs between the CDU and PDS,[57] which in terms of coalition building places the SPD in a favorable center position. But the SPD profits from this advantageous constellation with a view to potential coalition building only if it is successful in winning as many groups of voters as possible. The results of the last regional elections in Thuringia, Saxony, and Saxony-Anhalt, with absolute majorities for the CDU and a CDU/FDP coalition, demonstrate that the structures of the SPD that place the party at a competitive advantage by no means do so automatically. The ongoing pressure with regard to mobilizing voters, its weak anchoring in social structures, and its restricted recruitment of personnel (especially at the municipal level) contribute to the SPD's unstable situation in East Germany. It cannot be much of a consolation to the SPD that the CDU's situation is similar. In fact, the SPD in the new federal states corresponds more to the model of a professionalized media communication party, "electoral professional party,"[58] or "professionalized voter-party."[59]

It may be a little too early to designate the East German parties at the state level as models for the future development of parties throughout Germany. But the development of parties points in the direction of professionalized media communication parties. The formation of these parties is the consequence of social-structural and media change, which has been, for instance, accompanied by a slow dissolution in party memberships and the simultaneous loss of members as a resource for election campaigns, in addition to a professionalization and centralization of communication and a concentration on issues instead of programmatic coherence.

The gradual dissolution of party membership is one of the central challenges of the SPD. As is the case with the CDU, the SPD has recorded a permanent decline in members (Table 1); in the last ten years the number of SPD members declined by twenty percent. In addition, an increase in the percentage of old members is evident, while the lack of young people is dramatic. The number of young members in the SPD (sixteen to thirty) dropped from 10.8 to 2.8 percent from 1974 to 1999; the number of new members under thirty is below that of the fifties.[60] As Walter put it, "The majority of social-democratic members has turned gray and tired, they are more melancholy than certain about the future of politics."[61] Even though this negative development is true for all parties in Germany, it is especially noticeable in more recent SPD history because in the early 1970s the wave of new SPD members was mainly under thirty. The SPD has undergone a smooth transition from this structure of old members to the executive level: the party leadership is clearly dominated by a group of those above fifty, while younger members only provide a leadership reserve.[62] This generation gap could in the medium term pose a leadership problem to German social democracy.

Table 1. Members of the SPD

Year	Members
1948	844'653
1960	649'578
1970	820'202
1976	1022'191
1990	919'129
1992	885'958
1993	861'480
1994	849'374
1995	817'650
1996	792'773
1997	776'183
1998	775'036
1999	755'066
2000	734'667
2001	717'513

Source: SPD.

What further problems confront the SPD? To be capable of winning a majority, it must be able to perform the balancing act of integrating totally different segments of the electorate and responding to the moods of nonaligned voters who are influenced by media. This task has to be solved by increased public communication: in the future, flexible, differentiated, and permanent communication has to assume the role in social democratic majority formation that was previously played by the linking forces of trade unions and worker associations. These groups previously emerged on their own and were permanently regenerated in social democratic groups of voters. Forms of media communication with an inclination toward simplification, emotionalization, and symbolism will doubtless play an important role in the SPD strategy for mobilizing broad sections of the electorate. Not only is the incorporation of media logic and policymaking along aesthetic lines an integral part of the party's communication strategy, but also its ability to participate in public political discourse and use forms of direct internal and external communication. With this communication strategy, the SPD can prove that the demands on policy for both content and media presentation are not principally contradictory—that decision and presentation policy can supplement each other and do not necessarily have to move in opposite directions. If the SPD places too much value on media presentation forms, it runs the risk of demotivating its membership, of losing the substance of its programmatic identity, and of appearing in the end as only an "election campaign machine." With its strategic flexibility and its multifaceted appeal, which resulted in a favorable electoral positioning and coalition alignment, the SPD is in an excellent position from which to win future elections. But to keep this strategically good position, the party has to combine convincing public policy and governing strategies, social democratic identity, and a successful image through political marketing and political communication. Its public policy and governing strategies seem to be the weakest points.

Universität Potsdam

Notes

1. Forschungsgruppe Wahlen, *Politbarometer 04/2002*; Renate Köcher, "Angst vor der Zwei-Klassen-Medizin," *Frankfurter Allgemeine Zeitung*, 17 April 2002, 5.

2. Eva Kolinsky, "Das Parteiensystem der Bundesrepublik: Forschungsthemen und Entwicklungslinien," in Oskar Niedermayer and Richard Stöss, eds., *Stand und Perspektiven der Parteienforschung in Deutschland* (Opladen, 1993), 45ff.

3. Richard Stöss and Oskar Niedermayer, "Zwischen Anpassung und Profilierung: Die SPD an der Schwelle zum neuen Jahrhundert," *Aus Politik and Zeitgeschichte*, Band 5/2000: 3.

4. Franz Müntefering, "Demokratie braucht Partei: Die Chance der SPD," *Zeitschrift für Parlamentsfragen* 31 (2000): 337.

5. See also the empirical results of Thomas Poguntke, *Parteiorganisation im Wandel: Gesellschaftliche Verankerung und organisatorische Anpassung im europäischen Vergleich* (Wiesbaden, 2000).

6. Elmar Wiesendahl, "Parteienkommunikation," in Otfried Jarren, Ulrich Sarcinelli, and Ulrich Saxer, eds., *Politische Kommunikation in der demokratischen Gesellschaft* (Opladen/Wiesbaden, 1998), 447.

7. Gianpietro Mazzoleni and Winfried Schulz, "Mediatization of Politics: A Challenge for Democracy?" *Political Communication* 16 (1999): 249.

8. Ulrich Sarcinelli, "Politikvermittlung und Wahlen—Sonderfall oder Normalität des politischen Prozesses? Essayistische Anmerkungen and Anregungen für die Forschung," in Hans Bohrmann, Otfried Jarren, Gabriele Melischek, and Josef Seethaler, eds., *Wahlen und Politikvermittlung durch Massenmedien* (Wiesbaden, 2000), 24. See also Ulrich Sarcinelli, "Parteien- und Politikvermittlung: Von der Parteien- zur Mediendemokratie?" in Ulrich Sarcinelli, ed., *Politikvermittlung und Demokratie in der Mediengesellschaft: Beiträge zur politischen Kommunikationskultur* (Wiesbaden, 1998), 273ff.

9. Pippa Norris, John Curtice, David Sanders, Margaret Scammell, and Holli A. Semetko, *On Message: Communicating the Campaign* (London, 1999), 41.

10. Cf. Heinrich Oberreuter, "Personalisierung und Professionalisierung: Wahlkampf 1998," in Heinrich Oberreuter, ed., *Ungewissheiten der Macht, Parteien, Wähler, Wahlentscheidung* (Munich, 1998), 12: "The SPD completely relies on professionalization and personalization in accordance with American-style election campaigns as this found expression in the perfected media-effective production of the Leipzig party convention"; Stöss and Niedermayer, "Zwischen Anpassung und Profilierung," 5: "The election campaign of the politically-programmatically exhausted Union parties, conducted extremely confrontative and in the 'Cold War' style, was answered by the SPD with a professional campaign which applied qualified and clever mass communication methods to aggressively defend their reform projects." Franz Walter, "Vom Betriebsrat der Nation zum Kanzlerwahlverein," in Gert Pickel, Dieter Walz, and Wolfram Brunner, eds., *Deutschland nach den Wahlen* (Opladen, 2000), 229: "The election campaign was perfectly directed and one hundred per cent contemporary."

11. Matthias Machnig, "Die Kampa als SPD-Wahlkampfzentrale der Bundestagswahl '98," *Forschungsjournal Neue Soziale Bewegungen* 12 (September 1999): 20–39.

12. Matthias Machnig, "Von der Kampa zur Netzwerkpartei: Politisches Themenmanagement und Kampagnenarbeit der SPD," in Werner Albrecht and Claudia Lange, eds., *Kommunikationsstrategien für Non-Profit-Organisationen* (Gütersloh, 2001), 131.

13. Machnig, "Die Kampa als SPD-Wahlkampfzentrale," 29.

14. Machnig, "Von der Kampa zur Netzwerkpartei," 130.

15. Ibid., 132.

16. Peter Lösche and Franz Walter, *Die SPD: Klassenpartei, Volkspartei, Quotenpartei* (Darmstadt, 1992), 192ff.

17. See in greater detail Matthias Machnig, "Auf dem Weg zur Netzwerkpartei," *Die Neue Gesellschaft/Frankfurter Hefte* 47 (2000): 654–60; idem, "Vom Tanker zur Flotte: Die SPD als Volkspartei und Mitgliederpartei von morgen," in Matthias Machnig and Hans-Peter Bartels, eds., *Der rasende Tanker: Analysen und Konzepte zur Modernisierung der sozialdemokratischen Organisation* (Göttingen, 2001), 101–17.

18. Peter Mair, Wolfgang C. Müller, and Fritz Plasser, "Die Antworten der Parteien auf Veränderungen in den Wählermärkten in Westeuropa," in Peter Mair, Wolfgang C. Müller, and Fritz Plasser, eds., *Parteien auf komplexen Wählermärkten: Reaktionsstrategien politischer Parteien in Westeuropa* (Vienna, 1999), 392.

19. Müntefering, "Demokratie braucht Partei."

20. See Uwe Jun, "Inner-Party Reforms: The SPD and Labour Party in Comparative Perspective," *German Politics* 5 (1996): 58–80.

21. Andreas Kießling, "Politische Kultur und Parteien in Deutschland: Sind die Parteien reformierbar?" *Aus Politik und Zeitgeschichte*, Band 10/2001: 33.

22. Müntefering, "Demokratie braucht Partei," 340.

23. Machnig, "Von der Kampa zur Netzwerkpartei," 142.

24. Müntefering, "Demokratie braucht Partei," 340.

25. Ibid., 339.

26. Klaus von Beyme, *Parteien im Wandel: Von den Volksparteien zu den professionalisierten Wählerparteien* (Wiesbaden, 2000), 152.

27. Cf. Uwe Jun, "Inner-Party Reforms," in von Beyme, *Parteien im Wandel*, 37; Kießling, "Sind die Parteien reformierbar?" 36.

28. Karsten Grabow, *Abschied von der Massenpartei: Die Entwicklung der Organisationsmuster von SPD und CDU seit der deutschen Vereinigung* (Wiesbaden, 2000), 307.

29. Thomas Leif and Joachim Raschke, *Rudolf Scharping, die SPD und die Macht* (Reinbek bei Hamburg, 1994), 200.

30. Peter Lösche, "Die SPD nach Mannheim: Strukturprobleme und aktuelle Entwicklungen," *Aus Politik und Zeitgeschichte*, Band 6/1996: 27.

31. German Chancellor Schröder and British Prime Minister Blair signed a paper that was in most parts written under the control of former Schröder consultant Bodo Hombach and by Peter Mandelson, one of the closest confidants of the British prime minister, to outline a guide for a future social democratic policy. It is published under the title "The Way Forward for European Social Democrats." For an analysis of this paper, see Charlie Jeffery and Vladimir Handl, "Blair, Schröder, and the Third Way," in Lothar Funk, ed., *The Economics and the Politics of the Third Way* (Hamburg, 1999), 78–87.

32. Chancellor Schröder in his introduction to the report of the Commission for a new basic program ("Grundsatzprogrammkommission"), Wegmarken, 2.

33. Stöss and Niedermayer, "Zwischen Anpassung und Profilierung," 9.

34. See Franz Walter, "Führung in der Politik: Am Beispiel sozialdemokratischer Parteivorsitzender," *Zeitschrift für Politikwissenschaft* 7 (1997): 1318.

35. Stephen Padgett, "The German Social Democrats: A Redefinition of Social Democracy or Bad Godesberg Mark II," in Richard Gillespie and William E. Paterson, eds., *Rethinking Social Democracy in Western Europe* (London, 1993), 36.

36. Gerard Braunthal, *The German Social Democrats Since 1969: A Party in Power and Opposition* (Boulder, 1994), 350.

37. Klaus Dörre, "Die SPD in der Zerreißprobe auf dem 'Dritten Weg,'" in Klaus Dörre, Leo Panitch, and Bodo Zeuner et al., *Die Strategie der "Neuen Mitte": Verabschiedet sich die moderne Sozialdemokratie als Reformpartei?* (Hamburg, 1999).

38. See the detailed analysis of the parliamentary elections in 1998: Matthias Jung and Dieter Roth, "Wer zu spät kommt, den bestraft der Wähler: Eine Analyse der Bundestagswahl 1998," *Aus Politik und Zeitgeschichte*, Band 52/1998: 3–18; Wolfgang Gibowski, "Social Change and the Electorate: An Analysis of the 1998 Bundestagswahl," in Stephen Padgett and Thomas Saalfeld, eds., *Bundestagswahl '98: End of an Era?* (London, 2000), 10–32. See the various election analyses in Heinrich Oberreuter, ed., *Umbruch '98: Wähler, Parteien, Kommunikation* (Munich, 2001).

39. The very character of a government coalition with the participants forced to compromise for government cooperation gives rise to the assumption that the complete reasserting of the positions of a party on the government policy are nothing but an illusion. On the other hand, a government has to implement policy under more restrictive conditions than can be formulated by political parties.

40. Hans-Joachim Schabedoth, "Die deutsche Sozialdemokratie auf schwierigem Reformweg," in Wolfgang Schroeder, ed., *Neue Balance zwischen Markt und Staat: Sozialdemokratische Reformstrategien in Deutschland, Frankreich und Großbritannien*

(Schwalbach, Ts., 2001), 194. See also Wolfgang Schroeder, "Ursprünge und Unterschiede sozialdemokratischer Reformstrategien: Großbritannien, Frankreich und Deutschland im Vergleich," in the same volume.

41. See Wolfgang Merkel, "Die Dritten Wege der Sozialdemokratie ins 21. Jahrhundert," *Berliner Journal für Soziologie* 10 (2000): 102.

42. Cf. Frank Walter Steinmeier, "Konsens und Führung," in Franz Müntefering and Matthias Machnig, eds., *Sicherheit im Wandel: Neue Solidarität im 21. Jahrhundert* (Berlin, 2001).

43. Joachim Raschke, *Die Zukunft der Grünen* (Frankfurt, 2001), 420.

44. Franz Müntefering, "Die Politik der Mitte in Deutschland," unpublished paper, January 2002, 3.

45. Micha Hörnle, *What's Left? Die SPD und die British Labour Party in der Opposition* (Frankfurt: 2000), 468.

46. Cf. Uwe Jun, "Die CDU: Behutsamer Übergang in der Zeit nach Kohl," in Gert Pickel, Dieter Walz, and Wolfram Brunner, eds., *Deutschland nach den Wahlen: Befunde zur Bundestagswahl 1998 und zur Zukunft des deutschen Parteiensystems* (Opladen, 2000), 207–26.

47. Stephen Padgett, "The Boundaries of Stability: The Party System Before and After the 1998 Bundestagswahl," in Padgett and Saalfeld, *Bundestagswahl '98,* 94.

48. Gerard Braunthal, "The SPD Leaders in Power and in Opposition," in Peter H. Merkl, ed., *The Federal Republic of Germany at Fifty: The End of a Century of Turmoil* (New York, 1999), 121.

49. Padgett, "Boundaries of Stability," 94.

50. Cf. Ludger Helms, "CDU/CSU-Opposition im 6. und 14. Deutschen Bundestag," *Zeitschrift für Politikwissenschaft* 10 (2000): 511–38.

51. For details of the election programs, see Charles Lees, "The Red-Green Coalition," in Padgett and Saalfeld, *Bundestagswahl '98,* 174–94.

52. According to Joachim Raschke, "Sind die Grünen regierungsfähig? Die Selbstblockade einer Regierungspartei," *Aus Politik und Zeitgeschichte,* Band 10/2001: 26. According to Raschke, a party system consists of two dimensions: "an eco-libertarian dimension with the counterpole of authoritarianism and a dimension on which market- and justice-related values confront each other ."

53. Grabow, *Abschied von der Massenpartei,* 293.

54. See ibid., 172ff.

55. For the social structure of the electorate, see Tilo Görl, "Regionalisierung der politischen Landschaft in den neuen Bundesländern am Beispiel der Landtagswahlen 1999," in Brandenburg, Thüringen, and Sachsen, *Zeitschrift für Parlamentsfragen* 32 (2001): 94–123.

56. Andreas Kießling, *Politische Kultur und Parteien im vereinten Deutschland: Determinanten der Entwicklung des Parteiensystems* (Munich, 1999), 103.

57. To Kießling, the main conflict line in the East German federal states runs between the followers and the opponents of the old order (supplement 148 here).

58. Angelo Panebianco, *Political Parties: Organization and Power* (Cambridge, 1988).

59. Von Beyme, *Parteien im Wandel.*

60. Numbers given by Elmar Wiesendahl, "Keine Lust mehr auf Parteien: Zur Abwendung Jugendlicher von den Parteien," *Aus Politik und Zeitgeschichte,* Band 10/2001: 8.

61. Franz Walter, "Die deutschen Parteien: Entkernt, ermattet, ziellos," *Aus Politik und Zeitgeschichte,* Band 10/2001: 4.

62. Chancellor Schröder about Ute Vogt, thirty-seven-year-old top candidate of the SPD at the regional elections in Baden-Württemberg, who is also chairperson of the internal affairs committee of the German federal parliament. This title

could also apply to other ambitious young SPD politicians; for example, to Mr. Gabriel, leader of the state of Lower Saxony, Mr. Bury, state minister in the federal chancellery, or Mr. Scholz, party leader of the federal party in Hamburg.

63. Thomas Meyer, *Die Transformation der Sozialdemokratie: Eine Partei auf dem Weg ins 21. Jahrhundert* (Bonn, 1998), 101.

64. Sarcinelli correctly refers to the fact that the "rules of attention" by the media and the public and the decision rules of politics are not congruent. But policy has to satisfy both requirements simultaneously, that is, produce legitimation by communication and "legitimation by procedures" (Luhmann). The consequence of a one-sided shift would certainly result in a loss of legitimatization. See Sarcinelli, "Politikvermittlung und Wahlen," 19–30.

HUBERT TWORZECKI

Social Democracy in East-Central Europe: Success by Default?

In the parliamentary elections of 2001, Poland's ex-communist Democratic Left Alliance (SLD) won more than three times the number of votes than any other party, registering its best result since 1989 and simultaneously delivering a crushing blow to the ruling Solidarity-led coalition, which not only lost power but also failed to win any seats in the lower house of parliament. If at the time of communism's collapse someone had gazed into a crystal ball and predicted that Solidarity's heirs would suffer from almost continuous disarray and the SLD would emerge as the country's most successful political party, he would have been dismissed as a crank. For a number of reasons, ranging from the country's strong religious traditions, to a political culture that saw the communist system and its servants as a basically alien force, to a long history of political contestation of communism, culminating in the rise of the Solidarity movement in 1980, Poland was the one East European country in which such a result must have seemed particularly unlikely. Further, given Poland's singularly dismal economic performance under communist rule (hardly conducive to nostalgic feelings), as well as the country's relative success with market reforms in the 1990s, one could not easily explain the ex-communist left's electoral gains as simply the result of a backlash against the consequences of economic transition.

The SLD's growing strength (see Table 1) is thus the big puzzle of Polish politics, with clear implications for the rest of the former Eastern Bloc. It suggests that the ex-communist left may well enjoy some advantages that put it ahead of its rivals even when it competes in what would seem to be a culturally and economically inhospitable environment. But the SLD, unlike most other ex-communist parties, has done much to recast itself in a social democratic mold. This essay explores whether the SLD has been successful because of its ideological transformation, or whether the sources of its success lie elsewhere. It examines several alternative explanations, but in the end comes back to the issue of ideology. Ideological positioning is indeed the key to the puzzle, but not in the way it may appear at first glance. The sources of the SLD's electoral strength lie not in its social democracy, but in its use of symbolic and cultural divisions around religion, national identity, and the communist past.

Table 1. Elections to the lower house of parliament: Popular vote percentages for major political parties

	Election Year			
	1991	1993	1997	2001
Democratic Left Alliance (SLD)	12.0	20.4	27.1	41.0
Civic Platform				12.7
Self-Defense				10.2
Law and Justice				9.5
Polish Peasants' Party	8.7	15.4	7.3	9.0
League of Polish Families				7.9
Solidarity Electoral Action	5.1		33.8	5.6
Democratic Union/Freedom Union	12.3	10.6	13.4	
Catholic Electoral Action	8.7	6.4		
Center Citizens' Alliance	8.7			
Confederation of Indep. Poland	7.5	5.8		
Liberal-Democratic Congress	7.5			
Peasants' Accord	5.5			
Non-party Bloc/Support of Reforms		5.4		
Labor Union		7.3		
Movement for Reconstruction of Poland				5.6

Note: Only data for parties that obtained at least 5 percent of the popular vote is reported in the table.

Social Democracy as Adaptation Strategy

The substantial literature that exists on communist successor parties has focused much of its attention on distinguishing among the different political paths pursued by these organizations since 1989, seeing these paths as political-adaptation strategies that have been of crucial importance to the parties' electoral successes and failures.[1] A particularly useful typology, developed by Ziblatt and also used in somewhat modified form by Ishiyama and Bozoki, identifies three main strategies.[2] First, some organizations have remained true to their Marxist-Leninist heritage, especially in the sense of rejecting market-oriented reforms and retaining much of the rhetorical style and iconography of the former era. Perhaps the best example of this type is the Communist party of Bohemia and Moravia, which in its electoral campaigns throughout the 1990s painted the Czech Republic's economic reforms as a dreadful mistake and persisted with the use of red stars, hammer-and-sickle emblems, and references to Marx and Lenin on its posters and other election materials. Within the former East Germany, the Party of Democratic Socialism has pursued a similar strategy, though with an emphasis on the special context of German unification.

The second type of communist successor party covers those organizations that have sought to distance themselves from some aspects of their past, downplaying the "internationalist" aspects of Marxism-Leninism and replacing them with "national-patriotic" themes. Perhaps the best example of this type is the Communist party of the Russian Federation, which has combined sharp criticism of economic transformation with an insistence that communism—the communism of "true Russian patriots," of course—was not a foreign invention but a natural development stemming from the collectivism ingrained in the country's political traditions. A most extreme variant of this strategy was pursued by Serb communists under Slobodan Milosevic, who recast themselves as patriots leading the nation into a struggle for glory and territorial expansion—a path that ultimately led to war and genocide.

The third type covers those ex-communist parties that have reconciled themselves to democracy and a market (or rather "social-market") economy. Claiming inspiration from the West European social democratic left, organizations such as the Polish SLD and the Hungarian Socialist party have changed their rhetoric, their emblems, and their policy priorities. In their election campaigns, they presented themselves as competent managers who would see market reforms through to a successful conclusion while not forgetting about less fortunate members of society. Relying less on nostalgia and more on an aura of technical "expertise," they tended to focus on the future rather than the past, and on the West (being fully supportive of efforts to join the European Union, for example) rather than the East.

What accounts for the emergence of these three types? One of the most consistent themes in the literature on communist successor parties is the link between the character of the previous regime and the choice of adaptation strategy.[3] Kitschelt, in a typology that has gained wide currency, identified three major regime types in pre-1989 Eastern Europe.[4] The "patrimonial" type, found in the former Soviet Union and the Balkans, allowed for and was faced with very little contestation either within or outside the ruling party, and was characterized by personalized rather than bureaucratic-institutional hierarchies of authority. The "bureaucratic-authoritarian" type, found in Czechoslovakia and East Germany, was also characterized by high repression and low levels of political contestation, but it exhibited higher levels of bureaucratic professionalism than the patrimonial type. Finally, the "national consensus" type, characteristic of Hungary and Poland, tolerated a certain degree of contestation from within the party as well as from a well-developed (by Eastern Bloc standards) civil society. Kitschelt further observed that in national-consensus regimes communism ended by means of a negotiated process, in bureaucratic-authoritarian regimes through outright collapse, and in patrimonial ones through what he described as "preemptive strikes" by the old elites.

From the perspective of 2002, the correspondence between former regime type, transition mode, and the ex-communists' choice of adaptation strategy (social democratic in national-consensus cases, national-patriotic in patrimonial cases, and hard-line Marxist in bureaucratic-authoritarian ones) is quite striking. This is not to suggest that the development of successor parties was somehow preordained by the historical context. Nothing was fixed in stone, especially since most of these parties contained several factions and the choice of strategy was often the subject of vigorous debate. One can easily point to examples, such as that of the Czech ex-communists, who, even though they ultimately rejected the social democratic strategy after a leadership showdown in 1993, had certainly considered it. Nevertheless, the historical context mattered insofar as in different countries different strategies must have seemed more credible and more politically promising than others. The Czech and East German communists simply could not argue, as their Polish and Hungarian counterparts did, that they were reform-minded all along and that the social democratic path was a natural consequence of a liberalizing direction adopted long ago. Similarly, the national-patriotic strategy was simply not viable in countries where communism was widely perceived as something imposed from the outside and kept in place by the threat of Soviet military intervention.

In addition to the historical context, which largely accounts for the successor parties' early choices, several other factors that influenced the parties' political direction throughout the 1990s have been identified. Crucial among these is the nature of competition a party faced (particularly from other left-wing parties, if any) as well as the character, degree of success with, and popular evaluation of the economic transformation.[5] On the former issue, the presence of left-wing competitors limited a party's room to maneuver (mainly for fear of being outflanked on the far left), whereas their absence facilitated a bid for more centrist voters. On the latter, economic failure and mass hardships tended to push the parties toward hard-line positions based on nostalgia after the "good old days" and reliance on constituencies of the elderly, the unemployed and great many others who could not adapt to new economic circumstances. Conversely, successful reforms tended to strengthen liberal tendencies and allow communist successor parties to walk a fine line between appealing to the economically worst off and expanding into more centrist territory, attractive to voters whose economic situation was reasonably good.

To sum up, we know a fair amount about the reasons why communist successor parties adopted various transformation strategies that often involved a fundamental reshaping of their ideological identity. Much less has been said, however, about the relative importance of ideological transformation in producing political results, particularly when set against such other factors as organizational effectiveness, resource base, social "rootedness," and so forth. In other words, the hard question with regard to a party such as Poland's SLD is whether the new social democratic identity was the key to its steadily improving electoral performance, or whether other factors provide a more compelling explanation.

Poland: The Historical Context

In the late 1980s, the ruling Polish United Workers' Party (PZPR) appeared to have reached the end of the line. Fatally weakened by the rise of Solidarity in 1980, it had lost a third of its members during the course of the decade and was lacking in new blood and new ideas.[6] But its situation was in many respects a curious and contradictory one in comparison to its counterparts elsewhere in the Eastern Bloc, and much of this had to do with the uniqueness of Poland's communist-era experience. There are several factors that offer a crucial insight into Poland's variant of communism. First, even though the PZPR operated within the model of "democratic centralism," it always contained within it a number of factions. While not formally acknowledged, the factions were mostly tolerated, and even during the darkest days of Stalinism the struggle for ideological unity within the party did not turn bloody for senior leaders on the losing side. By the time of de-Stalinization in the mid-1950s, there were readily discernible "hard-line" and "reformist" factions vying for influence and hoping to give their own interpretation to what was described at the time as Poland's "national path" to socialism.

Second, Poland's communists seemed to lack the zeal not only to crush all dissent within their own ranks but also to reshape the broader society in a Soviet mold. They failed to suppress the Catholic Church, with the result that the regime's propaganda efforts would be continuously undermined by the fact that at least two-thirds of the population would turn out for mass every Sunday to hear a very different kind of message, based on an entirely different value system.[7] The PZPR also failed to collectivize the agricultural sector, leaving Poland—uniquely in the Eastern Bloc—with a huge number of private owners-producers who controlled about three-quarters of all agricultural land.[8] Perhaps most important of all, however, was the regime's decision after 1956 to tone down the system of mass mobilization, police surveillance, and political repression. As time went on and the Polish people became less indoctrinated, less afraid, and more willing to express their political views, the PZPR faced recurring challenges from various segments of a nascent civil society. In addition to numerically small (but intellectually very influential) circles of dissident activists, at various points much larger segments of society confronted the regime. In 1956 the challenge came from industrial workers, in 1968 from university students, in 1970 and 1976 again from industrial workers, and in 1980 from—it seemed—the society as a whole. While the exact numbers are sometimes contested, it is generally believed that from August 1980 to December 1981 some ten million Poles joined the Solidarity movement, including a third of PZPR's own members.[9]

This brings us to the third distinguishing feature of Poland's communist experience: the fact that the system, and the party itself, had virtually disintegrated in 1980, almost a decade earlier than in most of the rest of Eastern Europe. Seeing a mortal threat to their rule, the PZPR's leaders exhorted the cadres to an ideological counteroffensive against Solidarity—and nothing much happened.[10] The cadres, having grown fat and complacent during the corruption-laden 1970s, were in no mood or shape to act. In the end, Solidarity was stopped and driven underground not by the party, but by the army (which had retained organizational integrity and capacity to act), and then only because of the most thinly veiled threats of a Warsaw Pact invasion in the event the army had failed to act.

The end result was that throughout the 1980s Poland's political situation was deadlocked, with the communists too weak to reassert themselves and the broader society too exhausted to risk another round of confrontation. But in 1988, when signals from Hungary (where a regime-opposition dialogue was already under way) and the Soviet Union (whose leadership seemed open to new ideas) began to suggest that a negotiated way out of the impasse may be a realistic possibility, the PZPR's past practices suddenly became its assets.[11] And so, even as the hard-liners within the party's ranks looked to the future with apprehension, the more liberal faction sensed an opportunity: the things that made Poland's "national-consensus" model so unique could perhaps be put to political use. Democratic transition would not mean the end. Far from it, the party could run and maybe even do well in free elections if it emphasized that it (or at least some segments of it) had been reformist all along and did its best to liberalize Poland's communist system to the extent that circumstances permitted.

Still, given that the Solidarity experience of 1980–81 amounted to a truly massive popular rejection of the old system and its ruling party, what possible chance could PZPR have in free elections? A revived Solidarity would likely be unbeatable. However, as has been noted by many observers, Solidarity also had a major weakness. The movement was a product of very specific historical circumstances, a time when society united together in opposition to the oppressive ruling regime. The movement was rooted in an "us versus them," "good versus evil" type of moral dichotomy, which had immense power to bring diverse social strata together, but which would surely weaken once there was no "regime" to oppose.[12] Further, as ample survey data from this period have shown, even though Solidarity's members were united in their rejection of communism at an abstract, ideological level, they strongly approved of many of its policies (guaranteed employment, small wage differentials among different social classes and professions, state-provided health care, and so forth), and generally revealed a highly egalitarian set of socioeconomic attitudes.[13] In other words, one could have made an educated guess that Solidarity's unity would not last. There would be a natural process through which the movement would give way to a diverse array of political parties. And as the surveys suggested, in an electoral market that would be created as a result of this process, there would be strong demand for parties presenting classically "leftist" positions on socioeconomic issues.

The Transformation

In late January 1990, delegates to the PZPR's XI Congress, "conscious of [the party's] inability to regain the public's trust," voted to dissolve the organization.[14] By that time Poland's political transformation had advanced well beyond what was anticipated on all sides just a few months earlier. The story of this remarkable sequence of events is well beyond the scope of this essay. Suffice it to say that the Round Table agreement reached between the regime and the opposition in the spring of 1989 paved the way toward "semi-free" parliamentary elections in June of that year. The elections were only semi-free because the PZPR and its allies were guaranteed two-thirds of the seats in the Sejm, the lower house of parliament (elections to the Senate were freely contested). Nonetheless, the elections turned into a rout for the regime side and a massive psychological and political victory for Solidarity, which had won all the seats it was entitled to contest in the Sejm and 99 of 100 seats in the Senate (the hundredth one went to an independent candidate). As the communist dominoes fell throughout Eastern Europe later in the year, the transition in Poland gathered momentum, with the region's first noncommunist government being sworn into office at the end of August and constitutional changes (ratified on 29 December) that essentially dismantled the old system.

Given these fundamentally altered circumstances, at the conclusion of PZPR's final congress leaders of its reformist faction called for the formation of a new political entity, the Socialdemocracy of the Republic of Poland (SdRP). They were supported by two-thirds of the delegates, and so just a day after the PZPR's official demise a brand-new organization came into existence. A minority of (mostly older) delegates formed an alternative successor organization, the Polish Socialdemocratic Union, but it proved ineffectual and was dissolved the following year. The SdRP, by contrast, was dominated by younger people (the average age of delegates was forty-two), many of whom were previously active in PZPR-affiliated student and youth organizations.[15]

While this relatively "young" image of the SdRP would likely result in a political advantage, the key to successful transformation clearly lay in the ideological sphere. As its name suggested, the SdRP saw itself as a social democratic rather than Communist party, but a review of its key early documents reveals an ambiguous picture, characterized by an only half-hearted break with the past. In the first section of its founding declaration, the SdRP committed itself to the principle of popular sovereignty expressed in "democratic and proportional elections" within a parliamentary, multiparty system. At the same time, however, the declaration stated that Poland's evolving political system should move in the direction of "democratic socialism" and rooted the SdRP's ethos in the "traditions of Polish socialism, the contemporary explorations of the Polish left, and the legacy of Socialist International."[16]

The objective of this rather convoluted formula was to open the party up to the country's and Europe's socialist and social democratic traditions, but without fully renouncing its Marxist-Leninist, PZPR heritage. Such a renunciation was not in the cards for a number of reasons. Some were practical: the SdRP wanted to lay claim to PZPR's valuable material assets (especially land and buildings) and therefore had to acknowledge that it was in some way the PZPR's heir and successor. Other reasons were more personal: about 80 percent of SLD's activists had once belonged to PZPR, and whether or not they were actually proud of this, they had little interest in a strongly critical assessment of that period of their lives.[17] Still other reasons were political: it was already becoming clear in 1990 that Poland's political scene in the coming years would be organized around attitudes toward the 1945–89 era. Some of the new parties emerging from Solidarity not only denounced communism as an intrinsically evil, foreign-imposed system, but also, because of that, sought to portray people who once served it as morally unfit for public life. Consequently, they promoted the ideas of lustration and radical "decommunization," meant to complete the process of removing members of the former *nomenklatura* from positions of influence. Since quite a few people—not just the former PZPR members and their families, but many more individuals with complicated political biographies—rejected such a stark interpretation of the past and were threatened by it, a political party that provided them with a political home and defended their interests would be guaranteed a substantial and loyal core constituency. The SdRP, with its rejection of the PZPR's "mistakes" but acceptance of what it saw as its positive contribution to Poland's development, was in an ideal position to take advantage of this situation.

In the sphere of economic policy, the SdRP was sending a similarly mixed message. Its founding declaration spoke in favor of a "market economy with elements of state interventionism and social responsibilities of the state" as well as "equal treatment of different forms of ownership" (meaning public and private). It also rejected the "dogma that only private ownership is compatible with the logic of a market economy."[18] Its first full programmatic document took this idea further, defining rapid transformation to a market-based economy as "unrealistic, economically harmful and socially dangerous."[19] Further, it argued that the country's "economic infrastructure," defined as mining, transport, telecommunications, and the armaments industry, as well as tobacco and distilling, should not be privatized at all. The program also affirmed support for subsidizing (rather than shutting down) failing enterprises, guaranteeing worker input into company decisions, maintaining an extensive social safety net (described as being the party's "supreme value"), and preserving the "right to employment" that had been a part of Poland's communist-era constitutions.[20]

But perhaps most striking of all, a document produced by the SdRP's governing council in March 1990, stating the party's position on international affairs, affirmed its commitment to both the presence of Soviet troops in Poland and to Poland's continued membership in the Warsaw Pact.[21] Of course the SdRP changed its position on these matters following the Soviet Union's demise and later worked toward Poland's membership in both NATO and the European Union, but the document was nonetheless revealing of the party leaders' instincts and commitments.

While documents such as the ones quoted above would not be known to a wider audience, and would not necessarily contribute to the shaping of the party's public image, its election campaign materials certainly would. A review of such materials, however, reveals the presence of most of the same themes and much of the same phraseology. The "Electoral Declaration" and "Electoral Platform" from 1991 parliamentary elections, headed with the party's new Democratic Left Alliance (SLD) label,[22] repeated almost verbatim the statements about "equal treatment" of public and private sectors, the "right to employment," subsidies for troubled enterprises, and so forth. An election poster from the same year put it more succinctly, in big letters: "Work for Everyone" and "Free Health Care, Education, and Culture."[23] And the party's main slogan—"Things cannot go on like this!"—was a reference to the initial, painful consequences of economic transformation that included about two million unemployed and a significant drop in real incomes for most of the population.

The SLD's message in the economic sphere was therefore clear and unambiguous, and its thrust would have been arguably very appealing to many voters hit hard by economic reforms. But was it this message that accounted for the sharp rise in the SLD's support levels between 1991 and 1993? It would be difficult to make the case that it did because a look at other parties' election materials—even from those organizations that saw themselves as being on the right of the political spectrum—reveals pretty much the same economic message. Whether it was the Catholic Electoral Action (WAK) or the Confederation of Independent Poland (KPN) or the Center Alliance (PC) or Solidarity itself, all of them articulated critiques of market reforms and advocated measures that might as well have been taken from the SLD's playbook. These included "saving" failing state enterprises with subsidies of various sorts, relaxing monetary policy, and maintaining or expanding the system of social supports. In other words, even the most careful and diligent voter looking at the parties' election materials would have been hard-pressed to find much difference on economic policy matters between the left and the right.[24]

The SLD did well in 1993, proceeded to form the government, and in the next elections (held in 1997) ran largely on its record in office. Since during its time in power the SLD continued market reforms initiated by its predecessors, it could hardly turn around and criticize marketization in any blanket way. Besides, the reforms were actually beginning to pay off, resulting in one of the highest economic growth rates in the region. And there were political reasons as well for soft-pedaling a leftist economic agenda. By the mid-1990s, the SLD had become the political home to a large portion of Poland's new business class (especially the portion with *nomenklatura* biographies), which had little appetite for any sweeping redistributive programs. So instead, the SLD emphasized Poland's economic turnaround and touted it as one of its own accomplishments. Its slogan in 1997 was "Good present, better future." It lost (even though in terms of the popular vote it did better than in 1993) to a coalition of right-of-center parties called Solidarity Electoral Action (AWS), went into opposition, and in 2001 ran by seeking to project an image of competence and professionalism to contrast itself with what it described as an ineffectual record of its opponents.[25]

In sum, a good case can be made that in 1991 and 1993 the SLD's leftist economic agenda hardly stood out from the rest of the political field, and in 1997 and 2001 it was strongly toned down. If the essence of social democracy has to do with using public policy to mitigate the effects of market forces so as to help the less fortunate members of society, the SLD was neither the only nor even a particularly forceful advocate of such a position. Its Solidarity-led opponents were organized, after all, around a trade-union core, and despite their right-of-center self-image, naturally enough they espoused strong pro-labor positions. The reasons for the SLD's steadily improving electoral performance must therefore lie elsewhere.

Alternative Explanations

One often-mentioned explanation focuses on the strength and effectiveness of the ex-communists' organizational efforts and richness of their resource base. There is undoubtedly something to it. While not the strongest in terms of membership (the SdRP started out with some 60,000 members, much less than the 200,000-strong Peasant Party, but far more than the 10,000–20,000 typical of most post-Solidarity parties), the SdRP/SLD certainly had the most experienced political organizers, as well as a kind of natural understanding that "organization matters" that seemed to elude its opponents. Moreover, the perception of threat from a fiercely anticommunist right helped to quell internal differences and minimize factional struggles. But even though the SLD may have begun as a "community of biography," grouping people with pasts in the communist apparatus who had no place else to go, it did not stay that way. This core was later joined by others, mostly younger individuals with no "past" to worry about, opportunistically attracted by the chance of making a political career in what certainly looked like the country's most successful political party. And as to resources, there was indeed the helpful matter of assets inherited from the old PZPR, some of which were sold and others (buildings) that allowed the party quickly to establish a presence in most localities.[26]

That said, one could also argue that none of these advantages was insurmountable. Several of the SLD's competitors, most notably Solidarity Electoral Action, could also draw on a strong, "socially rooted" organizational network of a trade union and plenty of experienced activists. And as to material resources, in 1990 the parliament passed into law a system (expanded in 1993) of state financing for political parties that included free media airtime and reimbursement of campaign expenses in proportion to the number of parliamentary seats won. In 1997 the legislation was expanded further to include a direct subsidy for ongoing operating expenditures.[27] While resource differences among parties still remained, these subsidies did much to level the political playing field.

In the end, however, neither economic policies nor organizational factors can account for the fact that the left was able to expand its share of the vote from barely over ten percent at the start of the transformation to over forty percent in parliamentary elections and over fifty percent in presidential contests. This growth happened primarily because the SLD was able to present itself as a moderate political force, attractive to centrist voters. But moderate in what sense, and compared to whom? Two issues provide the explanation: church-state relations and assessments of the communist era.

On church-state relations, the SdRP/SLD from the very beginning took the position that the state should be "neutral" in matters of religion. At the practical level this meant opposition to religious instruction in public schools and to a ban on abortion, both of which were advocated by the church and most of the post-Solidarity parties.[28] More broadly, the left argued against the idea that legislation (including the constitution itself) should be based on and reflect "Christian values," calling attempts to do so a worrisome return to the idea of a single "correct ideology."[29]

Leaving aside the issue of whether the ex-communists, however reformed, had the credibility to make this kind of argument (it was certainly galling to many), one had to wonder about its political wisdom. Given that it had to struggle against the perception of being a successor to a party that served an alien system, hostile to Poland's national identity (of which religion was a crucial component), it seemed suicidal for the SLD to take a position of direct confrontation with the church. However, the Poles' attitudes toward the church were changing, and even though a vast majority still attended services, surveys began to show a marked decline in approval of the church's political activities and a growing preference for separation between the sacred and the secular.[30] During the communist era, with its rigid "us versus them" divide, the position of the church as champion of the nation's traditions was unassailable and largely unquestioned. But in a free and democratic context of the 1990s, and with the country suddenly exposed to the full blast of Western popular culture and its mores, some of the traditional aspects of reli-giosity and deference to the church's authority were quickly weakening.

The ex-communists benefited enormously from this shift in attitudes, all the more so that rightist parties chose to make an issue out of the church's role. Guided by the view of the communist era as a historical aberration whose legacies had to be expunged, they insisted on what they saw as a "restoration" of the church's place in public life. Religion in schools, chaplains in the military, a religious invocation in the constitution—the communists would have had none of it, so it was only right and proper that it be done now. Further, as the left gained political ground starting in 1993, the right's response was a return to rhetoric reminiscent of the pre-1989 era, portraying the SLD as the same old "godless communists" whose value system was inimical to national traditions.

The other issue that offered the sharpest contrast between the left and the right had to do with interpretation of Poland's post–World War II history and settling of accounts from that period. The SLD, unsurprisingly, took the position that the country ought to focus on the future rather than dwell on the past. It was mostly joined in this view by the liberals, who also preferred that a "thick line" be drawn under communist-era history.[31] The right, by contrast, insisted that communist leaders be brought to account for their actions, such as the deaths of protesting workers attacked by security forces in 1970 and 1981 and, more broadly, for the entire system of political repression. Further, the right saw a great historical injustice in the fact that many members of the former *nomenklatura* were turning into the main beneficiaries of economic transformation, and on numerous occasions threatened to conduct an "economic lustration" of the new business class. And at the most basic level, it was the right's position that people whose biographies included serving the communist system had no moral standing to hold political office or other positions of influence.

Conclusion

The left has succeeded by staking out a centrist position by speaking in shades of gray rather than in stark, black-and-white terms. As surveys have shown, this position has been an attractive one to many individuals who still went to church but felt ambivalent about the role that organized religion should play in a democratic society. Similarly, the left was attractive to those who—whatever their ideological orientation—were reluctant to engage in a blanket condemnation of an era that defined virtually their entire adult lives.[32] Poland's "national consensus" model of communism, with its relatively low levels of repression and ideological zeal, left in its wake a great deal of moral ambiguity and little public appetite for a crusade against its various legacies.

This of course raises the question of why right-of-center parties persisted with an ideological agenda that seemed to have limited popular appeal. The answer has to do with the basic problem of identity faced by the right in the postcommunist context. In post–World War II Western Europe, parties of the moderate, mainstream right defined themselves around the defense of middle-class values and economic interests. Offering a contrast to comparatively more radical proposals emanating from parties of the social democratic, socialist, or communist left, the right's message to its voters was one of material security, political stability, and reliance on tried-and-true institutions and ways of doing things. In Eastern Europe, however, given the absence of a conservatively minded, economically well-off middle class, the right has sought to define itself around much older, almost primordial themes of religion and nationalism, as well as the broad theme of anticommunism.

While perhaps unavoidable given the circumstances (the voters of Eastern Europe knew what their national and religious identities were; they were less sure of their economic status), these themes have in fact been highly counterproductive. They pushed rightist parties toward shrill, absolutist positions that found limited resonance in the modernizing, Westernizing, and increasingly "relativistic" cultures of the region, and have allowed the social democratic left to claim the electorally successful status of the moderate center, resulting most recently in its return to power in Poland (2001) and Hungary (2002). As time went on, party systems in these countries became less polarized along the economic dimension and more polarized along a primarily cultural divide having to do with religion,

national identity, and the communist past.[33] And it is this development, not the left's economic agenda, organization, or resources,
that offers the most compelling explanation for its electoral gains.
These other factors did play their role, of course, and it is true that
Poland's post-Solidarity parties have been exceptionally fractious,
riven by personal and ideological differences that stood in sharp
contrast to the relatively united front presented by the left. But, as
the 2002 Hungarian elections have shown, even if the right's organizational problems are mostly worked out by a strong and effective
leader, it still has a problem with producing a viable model around
which to define itself. By relying on nationalism, religion, and anticommunism, the right alienates a substantial proportion of voters
who, on balance, seem to prefer the ambiguous, muddled, and often
bland message of its leftist adversaries. What we are seeing in countries emerging from the "national-consensus" model of communism
is therefore not so much a success of the left, but a weakness of alternatives to it.

Emory University

Notes

1. John T. Ishiyama, "Communist Parties in Transition: Structures, Leaders,
and Processes of Cratization in Eastern Europe," *Comparative Politics* 27, no. 2 (1995);
Attila Agh, "Partial Consolidation of the East-Central European Parties: The Case
of the Hungarian Socialist Party," *Party Politics* 1, no. 4 (1995); Geoffrey Evans and
Stephen Whitefield, "Economic Ideology and Political Success: Communist-Suc-
cessor Parties in the Czech Republic, Slovakia, and Hungary Compared," *Party Politics*
1, no. 4 (1995); Michael Waller, "Adaptation of the Former Communist Parties of
East-Central Europe: A Case of Social Democratization?" *Party Politics* 1, no. 4 (1995);
Barnabas Racz, "The Socialist Left Opposition in Postcommunist Hungary," *Eu-
rope-Asia Studies* 45 (1993).

2. Daniel F. Ziblatt, "The Adaptation of Ex-Communist Parties to Post-Communist East Central Europe: A Comparative Study of the East German and Hungarian Ex-Communist Parties," *Communist and Postcommunist Studies* 31, no. 2
(1998); John T. Ishiyama and Andras Bozoki, eds., *The Communist Successor Parties
of Central and Eastern Europe* (New York, 2002).

3. John T. Ishiyama, "The Sickle or the Rose? Previous Regime Types and the
Evolution of the Ex-Unist Parties in Post-Communist Politics," *Comparative Political Studies* 30, no. 3 (1997); Mitchell A. Orenstein, "A Genealogy of Communist Successor Parties in East Central Europe and the Determinants of Their Success," *East
European Politics and Societies—EEPS* 12, no. 3 (1998).

4. Herbert Kitschelt, "Formation of Party Cleavages in Post-Communist Democracies: Theoretical Propositions," *Party Politics* 1, no. 4 (1995).

5. Waller, "Adaptation of the Former Communist Parties of East-Central
Europe: A Case of Social Democratization?"; Petr Kopecky, "Developing Party

Organizations in East-Central Europe: What Type of Party Is Likely to Emerge?" *Party Politics* 1, no. 4 (1995).

6. According to a survey conducted in 1988, only about 10 percent of Poland's senior-level communist *nomenklatura* was under the age of forty. It has also been estimated that in the early 1980s PZPR lost some 80 percent of members who were under thirty. Jacek Wasilewski and Edmund Wnuk-Lipinski, "Polska: Kreta Droga Od Elity Komunistycznej Do Postsolidarnosciowej" (Poland: Convoluted Path from a Communist to Postsolidarity Elite), in *Elity W Polsce, W Rosji I Na Wegrzech: Wymiana Czy Reprodukcja?* ed. Ivan Szelenyi, Don Treiman, and Edmund Wnuk-Lipinski (Warsaw, 1995).

7. Miroslawa Grabowska, "Kosciol W Epoce Przemian" (Church in an Era of Change), in *Polska 1989–92: Fragmenty Pejzazu*, ed. Miroslawa Grabowska and Antoni Sulek (Warsaw, 1993).

8. Andrzej Jezierski and Cecylia Leszczynska, *Historia Gospodarcza Polski* (An Economic History of Poland) (Warsaw, 1999).

9. Wasilewski and Wnuk-Lipinski, "Polska: Kreta Droga Od Elity Komunistycznej Do Postsolidarnosciowej" (Poland: Convoluted Path from a Communist to Postsolidarity Elite).

10. Marcin Zaremba, "Komunizm Jako System Mobilizacyjny" (Communism as a Mobilizational System), in *Komunizm: Ideologia, System, Ludzie* (Communism: Ideology, System, People), ed. Tomasz Szarota (Warsaw, 2001).

11. Anna Grzymala-Busse, *Redeeming the Communist Past: The Regeneration of Communist Parties in East Central Europe* (Cambridge, Mass., 2002).

12. Jerzy Szacki, "Polish Democracy: Dreams and Reality," *Social Research* 58, no. 4 (1991); Jadwiga Staniszkis, *Poland's Self-Limiting Revolution* (Princeton, 1984); David S. Mason, *Public Opinion and Political Change in Poland, 1980–1982* (Cambridge, 1985).

13. David S. Mason, "Attitudes Toward the Market and Political Participation in the Postcommunist States," *Slavic Review* 54, no. 2 (1995); Shalom Schwartz and Anat Bardi, "Influences of Adaptation to Communist Rule on Value Priorities in Eastern Europe," *Political Psychology* 18, no. 2 (1997).

14. "Uchwala XI zjazdu o zakonczeniu dzialalnosci PZPR" (Resolution of the XI Congress on Termination of Activities of PZPR), Warsaw, 20 January 1990. Reprinted in Inka Slodkowska, ed., *Programy Partii I Ugrupowan Parlamentarnych, 1989–1991* (Programs of Parties and Parliamentary Groups, 1989–1991) (Warsaw, 1995).

15. Aleksander Kwasniewski, the future two-term President of Poland, was the SdRP's first chairman. His relative youth (he was thirty-six at the time) added to the suggestion that the party was betting its hopes on a new generation of leaders. Miroslawa Grabowska and Tadeusz Szawiel, eds., *Anatomia Elit Politycznych. Partie Polityczne W Postkomunistycznej Polsce* (The Anatomy of Political Elites: Political Parties in Postcommunist Poland) (Warsaw, 1993).

16. "Deklaracja Socjaldemokracji Rzeczypospolitej Polskiej uchwalona przez Kongres Zalozycielski w dniu 28.01.1990r" (Declaration of the Social Democracy of the Republic of Poland Proclaimed by the Founding Congress on January 28, 1990). Reprinted in Inka Slodkowska, ed., *Programy Partii I Ugrupowan Parlamentarnych, 1989–1991* (Programs of Parties and Parliamentary Groups, 1989–1991) (Warsaw, 1995). All document translations are by the author.

17. The 80 percent figure is based on a survey of delegates to the SdRP's 1993 National Congress, as reported in Grabowska and Szawiel, eds., *Anatomia Elit Politycznych: Partie Polityczne W Postkomunistycznej Polsce* (The Anatomy of Political Elites: Political Parties in Postcommunist Poland).

18. Ibid.

19. "Socjaldemokracja Rzeczypospolitej Polskiej: Program Spoleczno-Gospodarczy, 1990r" (Social Democracy of the Republic of Poland: Socioeconomic

Program, 1990). Reprinted in Slodkowska, ed., *Programy Partii I Ugrupowan Parlamentarnych, 1989–1991* (Programs of Parties and Parliamentary Groups, 1989–1991).

20. All three constitutional documents from this period (1947, 1952, and 1976) spoke of a "right" to employment, which was often touted by the regime in its propaganda efforts as one of the greatest accomplishments of socialism.

21. "Stanowisko Rady Naczelnej SdRP w Sprawach Miedzynarodowych, 3 Marca 1990r" (Position of SdRP's Governing Council on International Relations, 10 March 1990). Reprinted in Slodkowska, ed., *Programy Partii I Ugrupowan Parlamentarnych, 1989–1991* (Programs of Parties and Parliamentary Groups, 1989–1991).

22. As the SdRP was preparing to compete in the first fully free parliamentary elections, to be held in the fall of 1991, it formed an electoral coalition with several dozen other organizations, of which the most significant was the All-Polish Alliance of Trade Unions (OPZZ), a labor federation developed and promoted by the former communist regime as an alternative to Solidarity. The coalition was called the Democratic Left Alliance (SLD), and this became the name under which the ex-communist left would henceforth run in parliamentary elections. In June 1999 the party formally changed its name from SdRP to SLD.

23. Election materials referred to here come from a collection maintained by the Public Documents department of the University of Warsaw library.

24. The so-called liberal parties (liberal in the West European rather than American sense), such as the Democratic Union (UD) and the Liberal-Democratic Congress (KLD), were the only ones that defended the policies of economic transformation, partly as a matter of principle and partly because these policies were largely the work of liberal-affiliated politicians.

25. "Manifest programowy Sojuszu Lewicy Demokratycznej" (Programmatic Manifesto of the Democratic Left Alliance), December 1999. Author's collection.

26. The issue of whether the state treasury or the SdRP/SLD was legally entitled to these assets was the subject of numerous parliamentary debates, several pieces of legislation, several decisions of the Constitutional Court, two presidential vetoes, and a criminal investigation. The results of all this legal wrangling have not proved conclusive either way; nonetheless, over the course of the decade the SdRP/SLD certainly benefited from taking over (or at least having the use of) a portion of PZPR's assets.

27. Marcin Walecki, "Dochody Polskich Partii Politycznych—Regulacje Prawne I Praktyka" (Revenues of Polish Political Parties—Legal Regulations and Practice), in *Finansowanie Polityki: Wybory, Pieniadze, Partie Polityczne*, ed. Marcin Walecki (Warsaw, 2000).

28. While the liberals (UD, KLD) preferred to side-step the issue, the only non-excommunist parties to question openly the "Christian values" approach were the Democratic-Social Movement (RDS) and Labor Solidarity (SP). The two joined together in 1992 to form the Labor Union (UP), which was initially conceived as a leftist alternative to the SLD. Eventually, however, the SLD's pull became irresistible and the two organizations fielded joint SLD-UP lists of candidates in the 2001 elections.

29. "Deklaracja Wyborcza Sojuszu Lewicy Demokratycznej, 1991" (Electoral Declaration of the Democratic Left Alliance, 1991). Author's collection.

30. Surveys by firms such as CBOS showed that the church's approval ratings had slipped from close to 90 percent at the start of the decade to around 60 percent by the mid-1990s. An overview of findings on attitudes toward the church and religion is available on the CBOS: <http://www.cbos.pl/SPISKOM.POL/1999/KOM078/KOM078.HTM>

31. The term "thick line" came into widespread use after a speech by Tadeusz Mazowiecki, Poland's first postcommunist prime minister and leader of

the Democratic Union party, in which he came out in favor of just such "moving on." The speech soon became a focal point of political debate between the right and the liberals, and was seen by the former as proof of the latter's "softness on communism." See Marcin Krol, "Ewolucja, Restauracja, Amnezja: O Pamieci W Czasach Postkomunistycznych" (Evolution, Restoration, Amnesia: On Memory in Postcommunist Times), *Res Publica* 5, no. 5 (1991).

32. An analysis of several annual surveys, conducted in the mid-1990s under the auspices of the Central European University in Budapest, revealed that about 80 percent of Polish respondents would consistently express a negative opinion toward giving religion a significant role in political life. Opinion about settling accounts with the communist past was more evenly divided, with about one-third of respondents in favor of "decommunization," one-third against, and one-third neutral on the issue. See Hubert Tworzecki, *Learning to Choose: Electoral Politics in East-Central Europe* (Stanford, 2002).

33. Ibid.

ROBERT LADRECH

The Party of European Socialists: Networking Europe's Social Democrats

Most discussions regarding the fate of the democratic left in Europe focus on individual parties in national political systems. Beyond this level, individual political figures have strode across the (West) European stage symbolizing the principles and values of social democracy; one thinks, for example, of Willy Brandt or Olaf Palme. By and large, though, when the health of the democratic left is assessed,[1] it is done so by counting the number of parties in European governments. This "counting game" does not evaluate the ideological attraction of these parties, but rests solely on the outcomes of competitive elections, which does not necessarily attest to the popularity of the winning party, and in many cases reflects on the deeds of the incumbent party. Nevertheless, the main point is that measuring the prospects for the democratic left has always implied a focus on the individual national political system. At the beginning of the twentieth-first century, it is now possible to speak of an emerging European left, that is, a political presence representing a common set of issue preferences actively trying to influence the decision-making process of the European Union. One of the organizational nodes of this political presence is the Party of European Socialists (PES). This essay aims to explore the PES—its background, organizational development, and capability to influence the challenges to social democracy. The attempt to form a European-level social democracy represents one of the possible futures for the democratic left in Europe. This is because the intensity of the European integration process has permeated so many areas of national policymaking. Indeed, "more so than at any point in history the fates of social democracy and European integration have become interlinked."[2]

Yet, as we consider the future of the democratic left, it is important to realize that we usually mean to say "lefts," and more specifically, national lefts. Although comparativists speak of common traits by which we may classify political parties into "party families," such as social democrats, Christian democrats, liberals, greens, and so forth, the variation among them owing to national circumstances has hitherto prevented the emergence of a strong identity beyond the national political system. In regard to Europe's social democrats, it was once remarked that "there is nothing the Socialists nationalize as quickly as socialism,"[3] attesting to the degree to which social democratic parties' practice in government rests upon national specificities. To speak of Europe's left, therefore, has always been shorthand for a collection of nationally distinct parties that nonetheless share a general common denominator manifested in rhetorical values and principles and a "genetic" origin in the nineteenth-century workers movements.[4] When we then speak of an *emerging* European left, it is precisely to indicate a European-level (relatively) cohesive transnational political phenomenon. It is the argument of this essay that evidence of this European-level social democratic actor is found in the development and operation of the PES. The PES acts as a vehicle for national social democratic parties' leaders to project common aims onto the EU policy agenda. It also serves to reduce the transaction costs associated with fifteen-plus party leaders attempting to coordinate debate and pursue common activities.

Background

The PES is the successor to the Confederation of Socialist Parties in the EC (CSPEC).[5] CSPEC was launched in the mid-1970s in anticipation of the first direct elections to the European Parliament in 1979. It was a loose confederation of social democratic parties that represented a first step toward bringing the various party leaders together in a routine and regular manner to discuss issues of the day *as partisan actors*. Although CSPEC was ultimately unsuccessful in developing a common manifesto for European Parliament elections that met unanimous approval, it launched the process by which social democratic party leaders began to interact on a European level and had, as part of their agenda, European issues to confront. Until this point, the main opportunity, of a formal nature, for social democratic party leaders to interact was the biennial congress of the Socialist International (SI). SI meetings, apart from the fact that two-year intervals were inappropriate for developing an intensity of interaction on pressing issues and the meetings were not confined to European matters, essentially operated as a social event.[6] CSPEC represented an advance by virtue of the fact that it had an organizational design that brought party leaders and others responsible for international and European affairs together in regular and more frequent contact.

This fact, regular and routine meetings of officials from Europe's social democratic parties, is important to consider for a number of reasons. First, development of a European perspective, that is, a supranational angle on issues that cut across national boundaries, or else shared problems requiring international cooperation, needs an environment suitable for the cross-fertilization of ideas.[7] Bilateral relationships have existed, having waxed and waned over time, such as the German SPD–Spanish PSOE relationship in the 1960s and 1970s or the SPD–French PS relationship in the first half of the 1990s. Nevertheless, the development of a perspective on what attributes a European-level social democracy should exhibit would necessitate a mechanism or forum by which debate could engage relevant individuals.

Second, as European integration resumed from the mid-1980s onward, with the Single European Act in 1987 and the Economic and Monetary Union Treaty in 1992,[8] national leaders began to recognize the necessity for a coordinated response to the challenge of European integration.[9] Although the European Union has national representation through the deliberations of the Council of Ministers, this is a body specifically arguing national preferences, not supranational or partisan ones. In the European Parliament, which began to improve its inter-institutional position vis-à-vis the Council of Ministers and the European Commission, party groups did indeed organize themselves according to party family, but relations between Members of the European Parliament and national parties, much less to national governments, have been historically underdeveloped.[10] Consequently, social democratic parties, or, more exactly, their leaders, had no organizational or institutional means by which to project and lobby shared views within the decision-making dynamics of the European Union. For both of these reasons, then, CSPEC represented, if nothing else, a "space" for sharing partisan views and enabled the development of innovative ideas with regard to the policy response by social democrats to the shape and direction of the European Union.

CSPEC was superseded by the PES in November 1992, at a special congress held in The Hague. A number of organizational changes were made with a view to making the new organization better adapted to respond to the quickened pace of change in the European Union (the drive toward monetary union had just been initiated with the Maastricht Treaty). One of the main features of the PES was its attempt to bring the national parties into closer and more intense interaction. This was pursued in two ways. First, a number of working parties on issues agreed upon as serious were established, where propositions generated could prove useful for party leaders, for instance, in the response to the relationship between monetary union and employment. Second, in order to bring a higher profile to the effort at creating a social democratic response to European issues (and also intensify the interaction of party leaders with each other), Party Leaders Summits were initiated, held on the eve of the biannual EU summits.[11] Although the popular press and media do not usually pay much attention to the declarations from these pre-summit summits, they have served a useful function in another manner. The preparation for these summits involves party leaders (or trusted associates) in the elaboration of policy positions, some of which previously may not have had much priority for some parties. Consequently, linkages are developed among parties and perspectives on issues are disseminated. Since the mid-1990s, EU summits have become quarterly, and so too have PES Leaders Summits. An additional aspect of these partisan summits[12] is the opportunity for those present, which since the late 1990s has included a majority of the EU's prime ministers, to attempt coordination of their bargaining positions in the EU summit.

The PES has served as a tool for national party leaders to elaborate a common approach to the impact of European integration in their respective national political systems, as well as in conceiving a positive input into the agenda of the EU. At this point in the political and institutional evolution of the EU, the PES as a transnational party is marginal in elections to the European parliament, and indeed in the daily legislative process at the European level. In this sense it does not resemble a "political party" as we understand their function in national political systems. However, this is not to say that it has been useless over the past ten years. In the following section I shall draw specific attention to the impact of European integration on social democrats, and then trace the involvement of the PES in responding to this challenge. This will shed light on partisan activity at the EU level as well as answer questions regarding the effect of economic and monetary union (EMU) on EU politics.

The EU Challenge to Social Democracy

The development of the EU, especially since its "re-launch" in the mid-1980s, has particular ramifications for social democratic politics, indeed for the entire left: green, communist, and so forth. This challenge to the left can be presented in two parts, the first institutional, and the second in terms of policy impact.

Institutional: The European Union has been accused of lacking transparency, accountability, and democracy. The term *democratic deficit* has been a shorthand reference for these demerits.[13] Briefly, the EU has become much more of a force in the domestic policy-making systems of its member states. However, the legitimation of these EU inputs is considered shaky at best, that is, the elected chamber that is involved in deliberations, the European parliament, is at best a junior partner in the EU decision-making process (although its position has improved over the past ten years). However, the other chamber that until recently monopolized EU decision-making, indeed acted as *the* gatekeeper, was the Council of Ministers. This body, composed of national ministers and essentially looking out for the national interest, meets behind closed doors and does not publish its deliberations or proceedings. Since the introduction of qualified majority voting in the Council of Ministers in 1987, it can be said that the situation has worsened in that the bargaining that goes on, which can potentially result in losers, cannot be traced to any one actor or actors, thus deepening the accountability deficit.

On another level, the institutional problem the EU generates has much to do with national democratic operations. National executives have been the "privileged" partners of the EU, the Commission and Council of Ministers specifically, to the detriment of national parliaments' ability to scrutinize executive activities.[14] National parliaments are not organized in such a manner as to have sufficient expertise and oversight on EU matters, and further, there is an executive inclination not to be bound by parliamentary constraints for purposes of bargaining within the Council of Ministers. National parliaments are therefore dependent on and beholden to their national executive to be brought inside the decision-making process.

Policy impact: There is yet, beyond this narrow evaluation of democratic deficits, another, and more significant, impact of the EU on national politics, and this has to do with the increased constraints on national economic policymaking. To put it succinctly, commitments to EU obligations, especially in the area of monetary policy, have reduced the scope of national government maneuverability. As pointed out above, qualified majority voting in the Council of Ministers means that any one or more member states are obliged to introduce into their domestic law decisions their representatives voted against. Second, these commitments follow a transfer of policy competence to the EU that can have far-reaching consequences on particular member states. The EU's Competition Policy seeks to reduce state aid to public and private enterprises and stimulate competition through measures such as deregulation and privatization of state-owned industrial sectors. For member states with large state-owned or highly regulated sectors (or monopolized, such as public utilities in France), the pressure to conform to EU mandates puts an enormous amount of stress on state and public-sector trade-union relations. The EU's Economic and Monetary Policy (EMU) also reduces the means that national governments have in managing their economies, and coupled with EMU's Stability and Growth Pact, even constrains what can be done in fiscal matters.

The discussion so far has dealt with the EU's impact on member states in general. What is the particular impact for social democrats? We can formulate the impact as follows: to the extent that social democrats are more disposed to seeing state action as a legitimate part of economic and social intervention, the constraints on national maneuverability have a greater impact on their policy development than parties of the center-right and right (by this I mean parties ideologically wedded to a neoliberal policy orientation). More specifically, the Stability and Growth pact limits on budgets, while prioritizing a stable monetary regime, comes at a cost for some governments for whom state-funded projects combating unemployment depend, for instance, the French Socialist-led government's thirty-five-hour workweek and state-sector job creation. The Competition Policy of the EU, clearly aimed at state monopolies in addition to private collusion, upsets the balance of relations between social democratic governments and their usual allies in the public-sector trade-union movement.

Finally, from a broader perspective, we need to consider the general economic policy orientation and that of Europe's social democrats. This is not so straightforward an enterprise. On the one hand, it is possible to summarize the EU orientation, taking into account EMU and its Competition Policy. Both of these policies were given their current lease on life in the second half of the 1980s, that is, coincidental with the "re-launch" of European integration and the Single Market program (Europe 1992). Apart from Mitterrand in France, most of the other political leaders of the then twelve member states of the then-named European Community were either conservatives—Margaret Thatcher, most notably—or Christian Democrats, some of whom were moving in a neoliberal direction at the time, such as Germany's CDU under Helmut Kohl. The "bargain" struck among them, resulting in the Single European Act, was essentially a neoliberal project, an exercise in what is called "negative integration," that is, the removal of obstacles to the free movement of capital, services, goods, and labor. "Positive integration," or the development of new institutions and practices to facilitate integration, was of a secondary nature. Social democrats supported the grand bargain of political leaders, and even more reluctantly the subsequent EMU in the 1992 Maastricht Treaty, because they had no common alternative strategy to put on the table. Projections by the European Commission on the level of growth to be expected from completing the Single Market suggested an improvement over the situation at the time, and so social democrats supported these projects. Consequently, we need to understand that as the 1990s unfolded, the "European project" was one born during the ideological ascendancy of neoliberal thought, and in the absence of a common or unified social democratic alternative, subsequent governments were obliged, as part of treaty obligations, to implement this grand economic strategy in their respective national economies.

The absence of a grand social democratic response to recession, stagflation, and the neoliberal onslaught of Reagan and Thatcher is not surprising for at least two reasons. First, social democratic practice had always varied from country to country. Second, the economic situation in European countries did vary such that for some, the logic of the single market was not such a confrontational project. Additionally, most EU member state governments are coalitions, and compromise is the norm. Intransigent opposition is not always the most optimum course of action. And finally, in some circles, social democrats came to believe that a post-Keynesian environment was now a fait accompli, and working within a neoliberal environment, and making the best of it, was the unfortunate duty of parties of government.[15] Finally, taking into consideration this state of affairs, and also the fact that for national-specific reasons social democratic parties managed by the latter 1990s to form a large majority of EU member-state governments, we have the situation where even if social democrats were to focus their energies and develop a common program, they were ill-positioned to do anything about it. For in addition to the reason that they were already obliged to respect prior treaty provisions, the EU is constructed in such a way that it is near impossible to introduce an alternative partisan orientation.

To the extent major initiatives are introduced in the EU, it is dependent upon national (or intergovernmental) interest convergence and cooperation. Whether deriving from the Franco-German relationship[16] or coalitions of key actors from business and certain governments,[17] the direction of the EU's policy identity highlights the continuing critical position of national governments in European integration. Put another way, national interests rather than partisan ones have been the source of historic developments in the EU. Coupled with the fact that the institutional arrangement of the EU decision and policy-making system has little outlet for partisan mobilization (apart from the European parliament), even if social democrats had a plan with which to alter the logic of European integration at the end of the twentieth century, they did not have a conducive institutional environment. This is the main point of this part of the argument, namely, for parties whose ideological program depended upon deregulatory initiatives and tight money policies, the EU was an ally, and consequently their objectives in this regard were being met. However, for social democrats, even if they eventually accepted that monetary union had *some* positive aspects, ranging from the economic to the political,[18] they had a limited capacity to influence further the means and future composition of monetary and fiscal policy at the European level.

In the next section I shall present briefly the actual response of social democrats as they attempted to overcome this marginalization of partisan agency. The development of the PES represents an attempt to develop a novel form of organization, one that will be labeled network facilitator. Its story also highlights the continuing divergence between the desire for a European-level environment conducive for national pursuits of social democratic policy and the reluctance to transfer real power to this level of policymaking for fear of continuing the emasculation of national parties as purposive actors in national governance.

The PES in Action

It is fair to say that the PES evolved during the 1990s in tandem with the rise in saliency of EU issues directly significant for social democratic parties. Therefore we should understand the PES as a tool for national parties to help them devise and coordinate a response to these issues. As monetary union was the central preoccupation of most EU member states throughout the 1990s,[19] it is not surprising that a prime area for consideration by social democratic party leaders would be employment. After all, monetary union was premised on the understanding that a stable monetary foundation and thus low inflation would help stimulate economic growth. Social democrats, having signed up to EMU, now wanted to ensure that employment generation was not simply an afterthought of the EU, but rather a central goal that EMU was to promote. Inscribing employment, however, into the EU treaties was not an easy task, for as stated above, national interests drive new initiatives. Those governments of a decidedly neoliberal character—the U.K. until 1997—would oppose any direct attempt to dilute the "free market" orientation of the Treaty on EMU.

The PES, immediately upon its formation in 1992, was in fact given the task of coordinating a social democratic response to EMU. This process, which unfolded over the next several years, attained a victory of sorts with the insertion of an Employment Chapter in the EU Treaty of Amsterdam in 1997. The victory should be understood from at least three perspectives. The first is the limited nature of the Employment Chapter itself. Second, the fact that the PES was used in such a way as to facilitate common agreement and efforts on the part of fifteen party leaders, many of whom were prime ministers. (Their ranks were added to on the eve of the Amsterdam Treaty signing summit by the electoral victories of Labour in the U.K. and the Socialists and coalition partners in France.) Finally, the victory reflects the continuing challenge to social democrats to balance their national and supranational priorities, and in this context we are speaking of the future of social democracy and European integration.

The Employment Chapter:
PES Networking Behind the Scenes

The Treaty of Amsterdam introduced a new Employment Title (VIII) making "a high level of employment" an EU "objective and provides for coordination and monitoring of national employment policies."[20] Article 2 in the Amsterdam Treaty states that employment is "a matter of common concern" and calls for the member states and the EU to "work toward developing a coordinated strategy for employment."[21] "Given the legal basis and the set of procedures which have been institutionalized in order to accomplish this goal, employment is now firmly established as a priority on the agenda of the European Union and unlikely to diminish in importance in the foreseeable future."[22] The Employment Chapter is itself a first in terms of introducing a policy onto the general neoliberal economic logic of the EU, but modest in terms of essentially coordinating national efforts. According to Leibfried and Pierson, "The provisions directly call for largely symbolic actions: the exchange of goals, procedures, guidelines, and reports. . . . The employment competence assigned to the EU level therefore is less about EU employment policy than about coordinating national employment initiatives."[23]

How did the Employment Chapter make it into the EU Treaty? Is it simply owing to "the alliance of social democratic governments, anxious to demonstrate their commitment (not least for domestic political reasons) to developing the social dimension of Europe"?[24] Certainly it was "supported by governments dominated by left-of-center parties and opposed by governments dominated by right-of-center parties."[25] But for a process ultimately leading to Amsterdam that can be traced back at least to 1993, numerical superiority at the last minute (the election of Blair and Jospin just weeks before the summit) tells only part of the story.

Working behind the scenes, that is, acting in such a way as to bring high-level party officials, and in many cases party leaders, together in the form of working groups, the PES coordinated the ideas and views of all its member parties to produce positions that could then be integrated into government positions and ultimately into bargaining positions in the intergovernmental conference that produced the Amsterdam Treaty.[26] A sympathetic president of the European Commission at the time, Jacques Delors, provided one element of thought on how employment should be brought to a higher profile in the EU's mission in the *White Paper on Growth, Competi-*

tiveness, and Employment: The Way Forward into the 21st Century.[27] Delors, Mitterrand's former finance minister, continued his partisan activities by supporting the efforts of social democratic party leaders to develop their own or support the *White Paper* goals. The PES itself was given, for its first Work Program from 1993–94, the mission of developing a social democratic European employment agenda. This resulted in the creation of a working party "of personal representatives of national party leaders, representatives from the Socialist Group of the PES in the EP [European Parliament], a representative from the European Trade Union Confederation, and senior commission officials (already engaged in the Delors white paper)."[28] The position initiated in this report and subsequent refinements became the PES' European Employment Initiative. This Initiative was clear in its recommendation for an Employment Chapter in the EU treaties. Space does not permit a detailed chronology of the various EU summits and Party Leaders Meetings that continued to raise the employment issue until success at Amsterdam.[29] What is significant is the fact that because there had been the intense coordination and development of thought on a topic that was, frankly, new to national as well as supranational policy-makers (namely, the operation and implications of a single currency and monetary union), PES networking enabled what could have been a fragmented and thus ineffective response by Europe's social democrats to the neoliberal logic of monetary union alone to instead begin instituting "countervailing" or parallel measures aimed at "softening" the EMU impact.

PES activities also provide an explanation as to why, immediately upon the election of the British and French parties, the Employment Chapter was ultimately successful in its insertion into the Treaty. The Thatcher and Kohl governments were opposed to anything diluting the logic of EMU (ironic in that Prime Minister John Major had kept the U.K. out of joining it immediately), and together would have blocked it. The fact that the British Labour and French Socialist parties had been partners, even though they were in opposition at home, at a European level with sitting prime ministers, such as the Danes, Swedes, Austrians, and Spanish, meant that there was little to no transaction cost involved in their "coming up to speed" on the issue of the proposed Chapter in the weeks before the Amsterdam summit. With France and Britain now backing it, and support for European integration initiatives in general, and for EMU in particular, the Germans were isolated and thus accepted the Employment Chapter.

The Employment Chapter was a success for European social democrats. It may not have been a revolutionary step toward social democratizing the EU, but it did prove that concerted effort plus national election success could be combined to influence the policy agenda of the EU. Concerted effort is the operative term, and perhaps only in exceptional circumstances can coordinated partisan forces influence the EU agenda, especially as it is institutionally structured at present. This is because, as Peters has suggested, political parties "cannot perform the function of coordinating policy priorities in the EU."[30] This is due to the fragmented nature of EU policymaking and the different policy styles in the member states. So, with this in mind, the Employment Chapter represents an extraordinary success for the PES.

The Employment Chapter episode symbolizes, however, another facet of the development of a European social democratic program. This is the reluctance of many social democratic parties to transfer to the European level enough power to accomplish certain tasks that, although increasingly difficult to attain solely at the national level, nevertheless still provide other forms of compensation. Simply put, "most social democratic parties want a powerful Europe, in a Keynesian manner, but most do not want to give it the political, and, hence, institutional means."[31] It is not timidity that prevents social democratic parties from pushing their analysis to its logical conclusion, that is, transfer to the European level what cannot be accomplished at the national level. As parties that still derive their power and resources from the national level, and with this basis dependent upon winning elections, to transfer some of the remaining levers that can be useful in national competitive elections to the EU robs them of legitimacy as purposive actors. If social and employment policy were EU responsibilities, what would social democratic parties have to offer their domestic constituencies? This is the conundrum for social democratic parties, for as parties of government (more so in terms of the probability of occupying national government than other left parties) who have historically been wedded to state action—"socialism's strength and distinctiveness lie in its strong conception of political agency"[32]—it is easy for many of them to transfer the notion of an interventionist state from the national to the supranational level. But as this depletes their domestic basis for relevance, and as long as the EU itself is not amenable to routine partisan influence through competitive elections that directly structure the work program of the European Commission, social demo-

crats support piecemeal change, hoping that their domestic electorates will credit them with success at the European level, as in the
case of achieving the Employment Chapter.

We can add at this point that although social democratic parties are arguably closer today in terms of convergence around notions of appropriate state action in relation to market forces,[33] there
are still enough differences and national specificities that prevent
them from agreeing on any centralized European competence that
undermines national management of their economies. So although
in principle most social democratic parties view some level of re-
regulation at the European level as necessary to balance the neoliberal
imperative for national deregulation and even privatization, in other
words support a "regulated capitalism approach" at the European
level,[34] European social democrats "have no common program for
economic regulation at EU level. Rather, the ongoing high-level discussions on 'progressive governance' seem to lead to the conclusion
that each country should find its own 'third way' suitable to its own
circumstances."[35] Social democrats are, in a word, caught between
the desire to remain relevant at the national level for practical purposes, but cognizant of the intellectual case for a maximalist reform
agenda at the European level, both economic and political.

Conclusion

A coordination mechanism of some type is necessary for transnational
party families. Although the social democratic party family may seem
quite a diverse set of parties, ranging from the Greek PASOK to the
British Labour party, its main competitor, the European People's Party
(EPP), has expanded over the past ten years to the extent that it
now encompasses traditional Christian democratic parties such as
the Dutch CDA and Berlusconi's Forza Italia! These transnational
party federations are important, in principle, because they allow a
level of interaction among national organizations that do not, on
their own, have the time or facilities to network across fifteen countries. The PES would have been invented sometime in the 1990s if
it had not already existed. The lowering of transaction costs is not a
benefit to be taken lightly.

The PES is a useful tool for national social democratic leaders
to project and even form a European social democratic perspective
on EU issues. As such it is not a unitary actor independent of its

constituent parts, the national parties. The Employment Chapter is one example of what could be accomplished within the EU policy-making system. Yet even an issue as significant to the identity of social democratic parties as employment was only pushed at the European level in a modest form, signaling the ambivalence of party leaders as mentioned above. The PES "itself cannot redefine national traditions and circumstances, but it has allowed these national perspectives to expand their horizons as the European dimension impinges ever more intrusively into their domestic situation."[36] This is the role so far that the PES has been given, that is, through the networking possibilities it offers to allow a space for the development of ideas outside the confines of competitive national politics. To this extent it represents one aspect of an evolving "European public space." The socialization of national party officials taking part in intensive PES working groups has potential significance for intergovernmental bargaining among the same individuals as national representatives.

At the moment, it is as a network facilitator for national party interaction that the PES functions most usefully. After the issues of employment and closer economic coordination, which seem to have proceeded as far as they can for the time being, the critical issue for the PES is enlargement of the EU. Viewing enlargement from purely partisan lenses, when evaluating the relative strength of those parties in Eastern Europe that at present are associate members of the PES, it becomes clear that in most of the new applicant countries conservative parties are ascendant. This puts the current slight social democratic majority in the EU into a minority, and potentially for quite some time. Consequently, a major initiative of the PES is both to lend as much assistance as possible to comrade parties as is legally possible, but also to inculcate in these leaders the perspectives of West European social democrats on vital policy issues that are and may appear on the EU agenda. Again, the presence of a transnational organization facilitates meetings with such a large number of new parties. The interaction of Eastern European social democratic party leaders with their Western counterparts, many of whom are prime ministers, also helps to integrate these parties as equals in the EU, thus going some way toward dispelling notions of second-class status.

When searching for a social democratic response to the challenge of European union, especially from the new context for national economic policymaking brought on by EMU, one can legitimately view the activities of the Party of European Socialists as one example. Within its working parties and the output as represented by Party Leader declarations, position papers, and the development of a common perspective on the pressing issues confronting the social democrats' future, the PES is a microcosm of social democratic possibilities. On issues of the institutional future of the EU, the role of European-level parties and supranational democracy, and policy most identified with social democrats, the PES is an active forum for debate. If we understand the emerging European polity as a form of multilevel governance, then linking the different levels—subnational, national, and supranational—across member states on a partisan basis is an enormous challenge. This is one key dimension regarding the future of the democratic left in Europe in the years to come.

University of Keele

Notes

1. In this essay, "democratic left" will refer to social democratic parties, whether labeled socialist, Labour, or social democrat.

2. Ton Notermans, "Introduction," in Ton Notermans, ed., *Social Democracy and Monetary Union* (New York, 2001), 1.

3. Ignazio Silone, quoted in Kevin Featherstone, *Socialist Parties and European Integration* (Manchester, 1988), 14.

4. See Christopher Pierson, *Hard Choices: Social Democracy in the Twenty-first Century* (Oxford, 2001), for a particularly perceptive discussion of the actual practice and identity of contemporary social democracy.

5. The PES has produced, available on its Web site, *A History of the PES: 1957–1994*, by Simon Hix. See <www.eurosocialists.org/upload/publications/37EN19_en.pdf>

6. This is not to say that the SI did not have working parties or did not take stands on political issues. The point being that the SI represented too general a level of interaction to generate a density of interaction needed to produce an influential presence on the international stage.

7. See the special issue of the *Journal of European Public Policy* 6 (1999), entitled "The Social Construction of Europe."

8. See Desmond Dinan, *Ever Closer Union: An Introduction to European Integration* (Boulder, 1999).

9. See Robert Ladrech, *Social Democracy and the Challenge of European Union* (Boulder, 2000).

10. See also Richard Corbett, *The European Parliament's Role in Closer EU Integration* (Basingstoke, 2001), and Tapio Raunio and Simon Hix, "Backbenchers Learn to Fight Back: European Integration and Parliamentary Government," *West European Politics* 23 (2001): 142–68.

11. On the organizational innovations of the PES, see Simon Hix, "The Party of European Socialists," in Robert Ladrech and Philippe Marlière, eds., *Social Democratic Parties in the European Union: History, Organization, Policies* (London, 1999).

12. It ought to be noted that the main competitor on the European stage, the Christian Democrat and conservative European People's Party (EPP), has also instituted party leaders summits.

13. See also David Beetham and Christopher Lord, *Legitimacy and the European Union* (New York, 1998), and Michael Th. Greven and Louis Pauly, eds., *Democracy Beyond the State? The European Dilemma and the Emerging Global Order* (Lanham, Md., 2000).

14. It has even been suggested that European integration "strengthens" the national executive vis-à-vis other domestic actors and institutions. See Andrew Moravscik, "Why the European Community Strengthens the State: Domestic Politics and International Cooperation," Harvard University Center for European Studies Working Paper no. 52, 1994.

15. Regarding social democratic internalization of neoliberal understandings of globalization, see Colin Hay, "Globalization, Social Democracy, and the Persistence of Partisan Politics: A Commentary on Garrett," *Revue of International Political Economy* 7, no. 1: 138–52.

16. See Alistair Cole, *Franco-German Relations* (New York, 2001).

17. See Wayne Sandholtz and John Zysman, "1992: Recasting the European Bargain," *World Politics* 42 (1999): 95–128.

18. See Notermans, "Introduction," in *Social Democracy and Monetary Union*, especially 2–5.

19. Apart from Luxembourg, all the other member states had varying distances to go in order to complete the EMU "convergence criteria" for membership. These criteria included bringing budget deficits down, cutting national debt, and lowering interest rates. See Kevin Featherstone, "The Political Dynamics of Economic and Monetary Union," in Laura Cram et al., eds., *Developments in the European Union* (London, 1999), 311–29.

20. Sonia Mazey, "European Integration: Unfinished Journey or Journey Without End?" in Jeremy Richardson, ed., *European Union: Power and Policy-making*, 2d ed. (London, 2001), 44.

21. Commission of the European Communities, 1997, *Treaty on European Union* (Luxembourg: Office of Official Publications).

22. Christine U. Arnold and David R. Cameron, "Why the EU Developed the European Employment Strategy: Unemployment, Public Opinion, and Member State Preferences," paper presented at the American Political Science Association Meeting, San Francisco, 30 August–2 September 2001, 3.

23. Stephan Leibfried and Paul Pierson, "Social Policy: Left to Courts and Markets?" in Helen Wallace and William Wallace, eds., *Policy-Making in the European Union*, 4th ed. (Oxford, 2000), 273.

24. Mazey, "European Integration," *European Union*, 44.

25. Arnold and Cameron, "Why the EU Developed the European Employment Strategy," 22. See also Mark Pollack, "A Blairite Treaty: Neo-Liberalism and Regulated Capitalism in the Treaty of Amsterdam," in Karlheinz Neunreither and Antje Wiener, eds., *European Integration After Amsterdam: Institutional Dynamics and Prospects for Democracy* (Oxford, 2000).

26. See chapter 6 in Ladrech, *Social Democracy and the Challenge of European Union*.

27. Luxembourg: Office of Official Publications, 1994. See also George Ross, *Jacques Delors and European Integration* (Oxford, 1995).

28. Ladrech, *Social Democracy and the Challenge of European Union*, 12.

29. Karl Magnus Johansson, "Tracing the Employment Title in the Amsterdam Treaty: Uncovering Transnational Coalitions," *Journal of European Public Policy* 6 (1999): 85–101. For the sequence of summits leading to Amsterdam in which

employment was raised, see Arnold and Cameron, "Why the EU Developed the European Employment Strategy," 5–11.

30. Guy Peters, "Agenda-setting in the European Union," in Jeremy Richardson, ed., *European Union: Power and Policy-making* (London, 1996), 67.

31. Alain Berounioux and Marc Lazar, "La social-démocratie dans l'Union européenne: Débat entre A. Bergounioux et M. Lazar," *Les Notes de la Fondation Jean-Jaurès* 6 (1997): 6–40. Author's translation.

32. Anthony Butler, *Transformative Politics: The Future of Socialism in Western Europe* (Basingstoke, 1995), 3.

33. See the various chapters in René Cuperus, Karl Duffek, and Johannes Kandel, eds., *Multiple Third Ways: European Social Democracy Facing the Twin Revolution of Globalisation and the Knowledge Society* (Amsterdam, 2001).

34. Liesbet Hooghe and Gary Marks, "The Making of a Polity: The Struggle over European Integration," in Herbert Kitschelt et al., eds., *Continuity and Change in Contemporary Capitalism* (Cambridge, 1999).

35. Notermans, *Social Democracy and Monetary Union,* 269.

36. Ladrech, *Social Democracy and the Challenge of European Union,* 129.

37. In addition to being from countries in which accession negotiations are taking place, parties must also have been evaluated by the PES as suitable in terms of democratic organization and policy orientation to qualify for associate status within the PES.

THOMAS F. REMINGTON

Prospects for a Democratic Left in Postcommunist Russia

Parties of the democratic left have fared surprisingly poorly in postcommunist Russia. The reasons for this have to do with the legacy of the communist state, particularly the weakness of organized social associations outside the state and the continuing strength of patrimonial and corporatist patterns of state-society relations, together with constitutional and electoral institutions in the post-1993 system that undermine incentives for a system of competitive national political parties.

By democratic left I refer to social and political associations with a programmatic commitment to pluralist democracy and guarantees of individual civil and political rights in the political sphere, combined with state policies that counteract the tendency of the market economy to exacerbate social inequality. Consistent with European norms, policies associated with the democratic left would emphasize social solidarity and the protection of vulnerable strata of the population against poverty, give priority to the provision of public goods over the dismantling of state-provided public services, and employ fiscal and monetary tools to redistribute income so as to reduce inequality. During the heyday of Soviet *perestroika* (restructuring) under Mikhail Gorbachev, many reformers hoped that it would be possible to overhaul the Soviet political and economic system in such a way as to combine continued state ownership of the most important productive assets of the Soviet Union with a pluralistic, competitive political system that protected individual liberties and provided society with institutional means to shape policy and keep policymakers accountable. As Gorbachev's *glasnost* policy evolved into the partially democratized parliamentarism of the 1989–91 period and ultimately into irretrievable economic and political crisis, the contradictions of such a gradualist path became increasingly evident. Although Gorbachev often made reference to democratic socialist principles, neither his institutional reforms nor his policies were capable of bringing about such a system and his efforts to reconcile the policies and institutions of the Soviet system with liberal values led to the collapse of the entire Soviet system. The nationalist movements in several republics—most important, Russia—could not be contained in any reformed federal or confederal model of the union, and the profound contradictions between market competition and the hypercentralization of the Soviet economic model proved to be too severe to overcome with piecemeal reforms. Most scholars would agree with the conclusion that the Soviet institutional framework could not be reformed into a democratic socialist state; a network of independent social associations integrating the diverse class and ethnic segments of Soviet society and aggregating the demands of a population that was abruptly given the freedom to voice demands was simply absent. Moreover, the bureaucracy could not readily be adapted to a change in political regime: it was heavily politicized by the demands for loyalty to the CPSU, sapped by corruption, stretched over immense territorial and functional spans of control, and, consequently, far more adept at insulating itself from effective political accountability than it was at delivering effective public services.[1]

The collapse of the Soviet Union in 1991 left behind fifteen nominally independent republics as its successor states. This essay will concentrate on Russia, asking why the democratic left remains so weak. Let us start by examining the relationship of state and society at the moment in 1991 when the Soviet state gave way to a partly democratized independent Russian federation.

Democratization and the Soviet State Legacy

Richard Rose has argued that in Russia, as in many third-wave democracies, democratization occurred before the state became modern.[2] The consequence is that people's new liberties are often employed in ways that undermine the state's capacity to enforce democratic and market rules impartially and impersonally. Lacking effective means to exert a collective influence over policymaking, many ordinary citizens continue to regard the state as remote and unresponsive with respect to policymaking, but treat particular state officials as susceptible to demands for personal favors or corrupt influence. Social relations in the post-Soviet era, Rose's surveys reveal, reproduce Soviet-era patterns of cooperation and exchange based on face-to-face networks of reciprocity rather than on impersonal ties to organized associations beyond family and friends.[3] Membership in social organizations is low, with the one exception of membership in trade unions. About 17 percent of the respondents in Rose's surveys claim to be members of a trade union, although this is usually a very passive form of participation; 90 percent do not belong to any sports or recreation club, literary or cultural society, political party, housing association, charitable organization, or civic group.[4] The fabric of organized civic life that would support a competitive party system is thus very weak, a legacy of the Soviet system.

Another consequence of the democratization of a weak state is its vulnerability to pressure from the newly powerful and wealthy interests that were formed in the early years of the transition. Studies of the postcommunist states by Joel Hellman and his colleagues at the World Bank distinguish three forms of pressure on the bureaucracy from private interests: state capture, in which the powerful buy influence over state policy; influence, which confers power to affect policy without necessarily involving corruption; and administrative corruption, in which individuals and organizations employ corruption to distort the enforcement of rules or the implementation of policy. All three forms are found to be prevalent in the Russian case. They tend not to overlap, in that the firms reporting that they exercise influence tend not to be the firms that pay bribes to get laws and decrees adopted. On the basis of a comparison of the postcommunist state, the World Bank studies show that it is the countries where *some* civil liberties are observed that suffer from the highest levels of state capture. Countries with low levels of civil liberties and countries with high levels reveal lower levels of state capture.[5] This observation suggests that those states where the bureaucracy was inefficient, unprofessional, and corrupt were vulnerable to allowing the new private interests that arose with the postcommunist transition to enter into corrupt relations of mutual parasitism, inviting the bureaucracy to profit from streams of rents at the expense of society.

Herbert Kitschelt's studies of the formation of party systems in postcommunist Europe offer a parallel perspective on the same problem. Where democratization occurs in a patrimonial communist state whose public bureaucracy has not become modern and professional, the patrimonial tendencies of the old regime carry over into a form of politics that emphasizes clientelism and the exchange of personal services rather than into a more programmatically-oriented party system. Parties compete for access to the state and the benefits they can provide, not through policy, but through patronage. Over time, modernization may enable social groups to demand a more accountable, responsive, and policy-oriented form of party politics. In the short run, however, parties perform poorly at aggregating the demands of large sections of society. Instead, parties are personalistic, machine-based, and permeable by special interests. In their comparison of the party systems of Poland, Hungary, the Czech Republic, and Bulgaria, Kitschelt and his co-authors apply this model to Bulgaria, but it fits the pattern of political development of post-communist Russia with some accuracy.[6]

It may seem odd that under Soviet rule Russia succeeded in modernizing some sectors of society while leaving bureaucracy in a premodern condition. The reason lies in the fact that the Soviet regime originated as a revolutionary, mobilizing socialist movement hostile to the hypertrophied tsarist state. Upon coming to power, the Bolsheviks pragmatically accepted that they needed to turn the power of the state to their economic and military goals, including a comprehensive industrialization program. But they created a variety of institutional devices to keep the state's administrative machinery subordinate to the changing political demands of the ruling Communist party. In the Stalin period, when the despot's personal authority largely replaced the institutional authority of the party, state officials became acutely sensitive to the need to appear to comply with the dictator's will, but also extremely capable at finding ways to avoid taking responsibility for consequences. Stalin's continuous effort to bring the bureaucracy to heel resulted in the recurrence of waves of purge and terror. Neither the revolutionary impulse of the Bolsheviks nor the personalistic dictatorship of Stalin was conducive to the formation of a modern, professional, impersonal state bureaucracy that could administer an extremely centralized socialism.

Moreover, the communist state was quite effective at destroying organized social life outside itself. The dense and vigorous networks of producer and consumer cooperatives, trade unions, parties, newspapers, workers' councils, craft cartels, charitable associations, nonstate educational establishments, and independent soviets that had formed before 1917 were destroyed or converted into "transmission belts" for the exercise of state power by the Bolshevik regime.[7]

Large-scale social associations were developed for the purposes of social control and surveillance.[8] Trade unions became remarkably comprehensive as membership organizations but exerted no independent political influence. They administered Soviet social benefits programs, mediated workplace social relations, and served as a convenient dumping ground for Soviet nomenklaturists whose careers had been sidetracked. They were part of the triad of social-control mechanisms through which the Soviet "social contract" was implemented (which consisted, alongside the labor organizations, of the communist party and the industrial administrative hierarchy). In return for compliance with the Soviet state's political demands, workers were assured job security and social benefits, at a low level of productivity and expectations. Trade unions proved to be incapable of exerting independent political influence at the point when large-scale industrial protests spread in 1989 and 1991 and workers instead formed new, independent labor organizations.[9] The very structure of the trade unions counteracted class or trade-oriented political action, since they incorporated all members of a particular industry, from senior management to the lowest-skilled workers. They tended to tie workers far more closely to the enterprise for benefits such as housing, medical care, recreation, and child care than to members of the same union or trade in other localities.[10] As Stephen Crowley shows, this pattern of socialist enterprise relations persisted well into the postcommunist era, severely inhibiting collective action on the part of workers.

These institutional features of the Soviet state help us to understand Gorbachev's failure to engineer an evolutionary transition to a democratic socialist regime. In contrast to the states of East Central Europe, discussed by Hubert Tworzecki in his article in this issue, collective interests and identities in the Soviet system were shaped by the destruction of class and other autonomous social associations and the power of residual loyalties to religion and ethnic nationality. In 1989, for example, when there was an explosion of strike activity in the Soviet Union, far more days were lost to strikes motivated by ethnic grievances than by working-class protest.[11] Self-interest on the part of state officials who foresaw powerful opportunities to control newly independent republics joined forces with nationalist movements led by the cultural intelligentsia in most of the republics of the union. When a referendum in Ukraine on 1 December 1991 produced a 90 percent vote in favor of independence for Ukraine, Boris Yeltsin and his fellow republic leaders immediately recognized the need to pull the moribund remnants of the Soviet state off life support and to declare the union dissolved. At that point the only viable strategy for coping with the massive breakdown of economic relations across regions and republics of the country was to launch a sudden and draconian "shock therapy" program consisting of the liberalization of most prices, the slashing of state spending, and as rapid a shift to private ownership of the means of production as possible. Implemented on 2 January 1992, with almost no preparatory work beforehand to build an administrative, judicial, and regulatory infrastructure to enforce market rules, the program was a self-consciously last-ditch attempt to restore some crude economic balance between demand and supply at the aggregate level. Much in the way that the Bolsheviks had seized power at a moment when the fabric of the state itself had reached a critical threshold of disintegration, so too the architects of shock therapy regarded their first task as the need to revive essential state functions, and only later to restore social relations to the point where they could relieve the state of its economic responsibilities.[12]

Given the revolutionary character of these changes, the early transition period in Russia could not have been less auspicious to the emergence of a democratic left. As Michael McFaul has argued, Russian society was intensely divided over the most fundamental political issues, including the definition of the state itself (whether the union should be saved or broken up), the nature of the regime (whether the state should be communist or democratic), and the economic system (whether state socialist or capitalist). The value of some kind of mixed economy may well have been widely shared among the public, but this hardly could relieve the polarization between democratic reformers and their communist and nationalist opponents that threatened to issue in civil war twice—once when the organizers of the August 1991 "putsch" sought to restore the Soviet order against Gorbachev's attempt to forge a new confederal union but were resisted by popular and military forces loyal to Yeltsin, and a second time in October 1993, when Yeltsin's enemies in the parliament and the radical ultranationalists and leftists attempted to mount a coup against him. In the desperate struggle for power, moderates of the left and right were marginalized.

It was only the adoption of the new 1993 constitution that allowed for the gradual development of political competition among parties oriented to peaceful democratic change. Yeltsin's decrees of September and October 1993 dissolved parliament but called for new elections to a new parliament under rules he himself set out. As dictatorial as his methods were, however, the actual electoral and constitutional systems he put in place were the product of years of discussion. They reflected a number of points on which there was already a consensus among a range of political camps.[14] Among these were the desirability of a bicameral parliament in which an upper chamber would represent each of Russia's eighty-nine territorial subjects equally and a lower, popular chamber elected through a mixed system of proportional representation and plurality/single-member district elections. Likewise there was widespread agreement about the adoption of a mixed presidential-parliamentary system (with the disagreements largely confined to the question of how much power the president should have vis-à-vis the government and parliament). Yeltsin's scheme supplied incentives to a diverse spectrum of political forces to enter the electoral arena and seek a share of power in the new parliament, even though the parliament's ability to shape national policy was considerably restricted by the fact that the president would have veto and decree powers and would appoint the government. Still, Yeltsin showed surprising self-restraint in the first years of the new system, evincing a willingness to accept some legislative acts that he initially resisted. For their part, both the communists and Yeltsin's supporters were perfectly willing to use the new constitutional system to push for legislation, publicize policy stances, lobby for benefits for constituents, and aspire to make careers in government.[15] The result was that the post-1993 constitutional order was surprisingly stable, and therefore conducive to the emergence of a democratic left as part of a system of competitive, programmatic parties. The puzzle, therefore, is that no such party formed. The Communist Party of the Russian Federation did not evolve into a social democratic party, and none of the parties that attempted to occupy a moderate leftist policy position succeeded in attracting more than a negligible share of the votes. To shed light on this problem, let us look more closely at the CPRF and the other parties of the left.

The Communist Party of the Russian Federation

Of all of Russia's parties, the Communist party of the Russian Federation (CPRF) resembles most closely the model of a European political party. Unlike any other party, it has a substantial organizational base, a well-defined electoral following, a large membership (estimated at around half a million), a large network of local party newspapers, and, probably most important, the heritage of communist party discipline, which it took over from the Communist party of the Soviet Union. It is by far the largest successor party of the old ruling Communist party of the Soviet Union (CPSU).[16] Its political faction in parliament is consistently the largest or next to largest, and it votes with high levels of party discipline. The party has preserved the CPSU's organizational structure, with a Central Committee and central staff defining the party's policy stands on major political issues.

The CPRF formed in 1990 as a reaction against Gorbachev's efforts to revise communist ideology by incorporating an acceptance of the market system. It was explicitly created to be the branch of the CPSU for the Russian Republic. Formerly, the CPSU had been divided into territorial branches in all of the union republics except for the Russian republic (RSFSR). There the party was organized into territorial branches at the level of the province-level regional subdivisions, including the ethnic territories known as autonomous republics, autonomous oblasts, and autonomous okrugs (districts). The reason there was no republic-level communist party organization was quite simple: any such organization would have been sufficiently large and powerful to have rivaled the CPSU itself. Understandably, Gorbachev strenuously opposed the creation of a Russian republic-level communist party organization, recognizing that such a party would have immediately gravitated to an ideological stance emphasizing Russian nationalism and social conservatism in opposition to the Westernizing, liberalizing, and pro-market program that he was carefully trying to inject into the Soviet body politic.

Nonetheless, the conservative opposition in the party rejected Gorbachev's demand for communist party unity and discipline and formed the CPRF. From the start, it opposed Gorbachev's reform program, identifying itself instead with traditional values of statism, patriotism, an aggrieved sense of Russian victimization, and hostility to liberal democracy. Characteristic of the CPRF's stance has been a consistent adherence to the amalgam of "red" and "brown" politics that manifests itself in antagonism to the West's materialism and individualism, a rallying around such traditional symbols of Russian patriotic pride as the army, the Orthodox Church, and historical figures associated with the strengthening of the state, such as Ivan the Terrible, Peter the Great, and Stalin. However anomalous it

appears from the standpoint of Marxist theory, in the Russian political context it is by no means odd that the CPRF loses no opportunity to identify itself with the Orthodox Church's advocacy of such
"Russian" values as collectivism, spirituality, and national loyalty.
Having abandoned the rhetoric of class struggle, the CPRF replaces
it with a staunch defense of Russian uniqueness—and, it goes without saying, the rejection of forms of globalization associated with
American mass culture.[17]

The CPRF's programmatic theses for its Seventh Congress in
2000 illustrate the mixture of Marxist and nationalist positions that
it avows. The theses declared that Russia not only faces the contradiction between labor and capital, but that foreign powers are seeking to impose their will on the country and break it up. It is necessary
to eliminate the "mafioso-comprador bourgeoisie" and establish a
new, improved form of socialism. In the immediate term, the party
seeks to create a mass workers' movement, organize more effectively
in the trade unions, and reverse the results of the predatory forms of
privatization that have occurred. Internationally, Russia should "play
a leading international role as a Eurasian leader and defend the interests of the countries of Asia, Africa, and Latin America from the
efforts and geopolitical aspirations of Western financial-speculative
capital."[18] Such rhetoric is characteristic of the party's efforts to
downplay the traditional language of the class struggle in favor of
nationalism and anti-Westernism.

The CPRF has succeeded in preserving its organizational unity
despite serious internal divisions. Within its leadership are moderate elements advocating cooperation with the government in making policy where mutually acceptable agreements are possible,
together with hard-liners emphasizing the party's oppositional stance.
The party has managed to straddle this divide since it first entered
the parliamentary arena in the December 1993 elections. Generally
its parliamentary faction is somewhat more moderate than the Central Committee, although within the faction are representatives of
the full spectrum of ideological camps in the party, from orthodox
Marxist-Leninists to pragmatic moderates to Russian nationalists.

The communists have been adept at maneuvering between pragmatic and militant strategies. The Duma's chairmen after the 1993,
1995, and 1999 elections had been drawn from among the ranks of
the communists in the Duma. Ivan Rybkin, a moderate communist
who had run on the agrarian party list, was elected chairman when
the first Duma convened in January 1994. In January 1996, after the

communists had won approximately 23 percent of the party list vote in December 1995, a somewhat more orthodox communist, Gennadii Seleznev, was elected chairman of the Duma. Seleznev was reelected chairman after the 1999 elections. However, both Rybkin and Seleznev became moderate and pragmatic in their relations with the Kremlin. Indeed, most observers have concluded that they were fully co-opted into the Kremlin's inner circle, becoming reliable allies of the Kremlin in the Duma rather than leaders of the loyal opposition. Nonetheless, however much some communists may have resented the fact that the Duma's speakers switched their loyalty to the president from the party, neither Rybkin nor Seleznev ever had to face a serious threat by their party to remove them from their positions.[19] Moreover, the short-lived Primakov government—which lasted only from September 1998 until March 1999—drew one of the communists' senior economic policy specialists, Yuri Masliukov, former head of Gosplan, into the government as first deputy prime minister responsible for economic policy.

In addition to participating in the government in this way, the CPRF in the Duma has often supported government-sponsored legislation; it has regularly voted for the state budget law, for example, after working to modify it as much as possible to maximize the support for sectors the communists took a particular interest in. It has routinely entered into political coalitions with other parliamentary factions in support of particular pieces of legislation. On a number of issues having to do with the strengthening of the power of the federal government vis-à-vis the governments of the territorial subjects, it has cooperated with the Kremlin. In general, the communists have been much closer to the Kremlin on federalism matters than they have on issues dealing with property rights, privatization, and economic policy. Certainly they have been eager to make use of the organizational and staff resources that come from participating in the Duma for the purposes of running their parliamentary election campaigns. Thus the CPRF has clearly been a parliamentary party rather than a party working to overthrow the constitutional regime.

In other respects, the CPRF has maintained a militantly oppositional stance to Yeltsin, Vladimir Putin, and the government. Periodically it has demanded votes of no confidence in the government, and for several years it attempted to find ways to remove Yeltsin (or at least embarrass him through impeachment proceedings).[20] A fairly typical example of the party's ability to tolerate both anti-system and within-system elements occurred in the summer of 1998. Viktor Ilyukhin, the fire-breathing communist chair of the Duma committee on security policy, called for removing Yeltsin by all mean necessary, "including illegal ones," to remove the Yeltsin regime, on the grounds that criminals "must be fought with whatever means at one's disposal, not those the regime itself has imposed." In response, the party's leader, Gennadii Zyuganov, issued a statement denying reports that his party aims to use illegal means to remove the current regime, and emphasizing that the party believed that "Communists and all patriotic forces" in Russia could overcome the "crisis" by working within "constitutional and legal norms."[21]

The communists finally succeeded in placing impeachment on the Duma's agenda in 1998. The Duma voted in June 1998 to form a commission to study a series of accusations against Yeltsin. There were five charges: that he had committed treason by signing the agreement in December 1991 to dissolve the Soviet Union; that he had illegally initiated the war in Chechnia in 1994; that he had illegally dissolved the Russian Congress and Supreme Soviet in 1993; that he had destroyed Russia's defense capacity; and that he had committed genocide against the Russian people by the effects of the economic policies of his government since 1992. Eventually the commission decided to drop the charge that he had deliberately destroyed Russia's defensive capabilities, but agreed to present the other charges to the full chamber for its consideration. The irrepressible Viktor Ilyukhin went further and claimed that the "genocide" against the Russian people would have been less if among the president's entourage there "had predominated people of the indigenous nationality, and not the Jewish nation alone, although this nation by itself is talented." Rather than to disavow this and other anti-Semitic utterances by some of its members, the communist party faction's response to the immediate outcry was to accuse the mass media of distorting Ilyukhin's remarks.

In March 1999 the commission approved all five charges and submitted them to the full chamber for its consideration. The Duma began debate on impeachment on 13 May 1999, and on 15 May voted on the five charges. Although the third charge came close, none gained the required 300 votes. The anticlimactic nature of the impeachment vote was reinforced by the fact that, although the president had chosen the eve of the debate—12 May—to dismiss the government yet again, the Duma went along with Sergei Stepashin's nomination as Primakov's successor and approved Stepashin's appointment by 301 votes to 55.[22]

The CPRF has thus managed to avoid an outright split between its moderate and hard-line wings, although frequently tensions between the two tendencies are revealed publicly.[23] The consequence of preserving a public face of unity, however, is severe ideologically and institutional rigidity. The party has been unable to move decisively either in the direction of a social democratic, moderate stance or toward more orthodox Marxism-Leninism. It is ideologically straitjacketed: if it moves too much to the center of the political spectrum, it will lose its distinctiveness as a clear alternative to the government, but if it moves further to the left, it will marginalize itself. Papering over this perennial tension with the rhetoric of Russian nationalism and patriotism, the party has been unable to broaden its electoral base. Its voters tend to be older than average, and it appeals to them by associating itself with the positive aspects of the old regime (the comprehensive social safety net, the victory in World War II, the imperial power and reach of the union state). The result is that the CPRF has a rather stable share of the electorate, but one which (so far, at least) prevents it from winning a majority in parliament or capturing the presidency. In 1993, it took 12.4 percent of the party list vote; in 1995, 22.7 percent; and in 1999, 24.29 percent. In presidential elections, its leader, Gennadii Ziuganov, is the perennial runner-up: in 1996, Ziuganov won 32 percent of the vote in the first round and 40.3 percent in the second; in 2000, he took 29.2 percent. Surveys of voters show that the communists consistently are preferred by around one-third of the voters to other parties, and their support sometimes reaches close to 40 percent of the electorate.[24] It is safe to conclude that the same factors of ideology, reputation, and organization that give the communists a consistent base level of electoral support also limit their chances for expanding their political influence or altering their policy position.[25]

Alternatives on the Left

Yabloko

There are other parties that might fill the role of a democratic left. One is the party Yabloko. Yabloko was formed initially to compete in the 1993 elections and has remained a small but stable programmatic alternative both to the communists and to the government. Headed by economist Grigorii Yavlinskii, the Yabloko party has staked out a niche in which it claims to offer a democratic alterna-

tive to the neoliberalism of the Yeltsin and Putin governments and
to the extremism and authoritarianism of the communists. Yavlinskii
has consistently refused to enter government on any but his own
terms, so his criticism of policy enjoys the advantage of being un-
contaminated by executive responsibility. In the Duma, the Yabloko
faction has been one of the most active in proposing legislation. It
has worked on a variety of issues, including social welfare policy,
federalism, and electoral reform. Its general line is in favor of market-oriented reform, but with a strong emphasis on social protection. It is a defender of civil and political rights—taking a strong
and unpopular stance against the government's wars in Chechnia,
for instance—and favors closer contact between Russia and the West.

Yabloko's electoral following is relatively narrow, although its
vote share has been stable throughout the decade. In 1993, the party
received 7.86 percent of the party list vote, 7.0 percent in 1995, and
5.8 percent in 1999. Running for president, Yavlinskii received about
7 percent of the vote in 1996 and 5.8 percent in 1999. Public opinion surveys by the All-Russian Institute for the Study of Public Opinion (VTsIOM, for its Russian initials) indicate that since 2000,
Yabloko's support has never exceeded 10 percent nor fallen below 7
percent.[26] Yabloko draws most strongly in a few regions, particularly
St. Petersburg and Moscow, and from among educated groups of the
population. Like the communists, it has been unable to break outside of this relatively limited but loyal constituency and become a
serious contender for national power. In 2000 it announced that it
was forming a political alliance with its free-market rivals, the Union
of Right Forces. However, this alliance has foundered as the right-
ists have entered into closer relations with Putin's government in
developing a large body of market-oriented legislation and Yabloko
has been unwilling to follow suit.

The Social Democratic Party

Former President Mikhail Gorbachev heads a very small party called
the Russian Social Democratic Party. In spring 2001, with President
Putin's encouragement, Gorbachev's party united with several other
even smaller parties to form the United Social Democratic Party of
Russia. Gorbachev's desire to maintain cooperative relations with
President Putin was evident in his comments that Putin's policies
generally reflected the interests of the social democrats and that Putin
himself had told him, in a private conversation, of "his sympathy

toward social democrats."[27] How interested Putin was in encouraging a serious social democratic party was another matter, although undoubtedly Putin would like to see the social democratic party weaken support for the communists. The likelihood that Gorbachev's party could draw off any significant share of the communist vote is very low, however. VTsIOM polls indicate that the party has the support of only one percent of the electorate.[28] In the 1999 election, three parties claimed the socialist or social democratic banner: the Social Democratic Party, the Socialist Party of Russia, and the Russian Socialist Party. Together they won only four-tenths of a percent of the party list vote.

Periodically the Kremlin's political managers attempt to create a moderate leftist alternative to the CPRF. Encouraging Gorbachev to unite several small parties under the banner of his social democratic party is one example. Another was an effort in 1995 to form a coalition of small socialist and social democratic parties around Duma speaker Ivan Rybkin. This bloc—called the bloc of Ivan Rybkin—performed dismally in the 1995 election, however, receiving only 1.1 percent of the vote. In the spring of 2000, the Kremlin attempted to create another such bloc, called "Rossiia" (Russia), again organized around the figure of the Duma chairman. The Russian press speculated that Rossiia was a Kremlin-inspired effort to split the CPRF and create a social democratic party. At one point it appeared that Rossiia might be able to draw off a significant share of the CPRF's organizational base. Seleznev himself called it an attempt to create a "center-left movement" for people who were neither communists nor social democrats. But at the same time, Seleznev was unwilling to cut his ties to the CPRF and insisted that the new movement was not a party.[29] Whatever the Kremlin's intentions, the new movement was soon forgotten.

Obstacles to the Formation of a Party System

As these examples indicate, attempts to use the executive branch's administrative levers to form moderate left parties have failed, while the CPRF has remained locked in a programmatic stance that assures it about a third of the electorate's support but prevents it from evolving into a social democratic party. Factors associated with the inheritance of the communist system help explain this pattern: the centralization of state power and weakness of civil society, and the patrimonial and corporatist character of social relations inhibiting class-based collective action, remain significant features of the postcommunist system. The poverty of aggregating institutions throughout society makes parties highly dependent on state resources. As a result, they are far more strongly developed as parliamentary factions than as electoral organizations. Moreover, the pattern of development of the early postcommunist transition affected business and labor differently. Business interests were able to organize through inherited associations of state enterprise managers, such as the Russian Union of Industrialists and Entrepreneurs, and new start-up organizations, such as the Bankers' Association. Labor, however, found that the formerly unified umbrella federation of trade unions, renamed the Federation of Independent Trade Unions of Russia, could not maintain its unity in the face of divisions across regions and sectors. Different regional and sectoral branches of the FITUR formed their own political alliances, while at the workplace level workers remained dependent on their enterprises for their social benefits. The trade union organization persisted in its dependent and docile relationship to the state rather than becoming an autonomous social interest capable of supporting a democratic left political movement.

As important as the Soviet legacy is, however, in understanding the forms of social and state organization, other factors specific to the post-1993 constitutional and electoral system undercut the possibility that a viable party system can arise. Two features of the institutional environment in particular stand out. One is the way in which the electoral system combines proportional representation elements with plurality/single-member district representation. The other is the way in which the Russian constitution combines presidential and parliamentary elements.

The electoral system used for Duma elections divides the 450 seats in the Duma into two categories: those filled by elections using proportional representation in a single national electoral district from parties whose lists have received at least 5 percent of the vote, and those filled by plurality winners of races in 225 single-member districts. In contrast to the system used in Germany, Russia's electoral system provides no compensation seats. The two categories of seats are filled separately. Once elected, single-member district deputies tend either to join the parliamentary factions created by the parties whose list candidates have won seats or to form their own factions made up of independents. Because the overall proportions of party representation in the chamber are not set to equal the proportions of votes won by parties in the party list ballot (as they are in Germany), single-member district deputies often find it preferable to join such independent groups rather than to enter one of the party-based factions.

Moreover, as Olga Shvetsova has argued, such a mixed system has paradoxical results. It tends to undermine incentives for forming coalitions. Smaller parties often reason that they can use the free media exposure that they can obtain by registering as party lists in the PR portion of the ballot in order to run select candidates in single-member district races, which may be more attractive to them than submerging their organizations into larger parties. By the same token, parties calculating that they can clear the 5 percent threshold in the party list ballot do not face the pressures to unite behind a single party that they would (as in the logic of Duverger's law) in a pure SMD system. The result is a continuing fragmentation of the party system.[30]

The other problem is the power of the president to name the government. The president is not directly required to ensure that the government reflects the balance of party forces in parliament. Although nothing in the constitution prevents the president from appointing a party-based government, neither the constitution nor precedent requires him to do so. Yeltsin's practice, continued by Putin, has been to name a government made up largely of officials with no party ties whose careers for the most part have been in the executive branch rather than in parliamentary politics. The only requirement is that the prime minister be confirmed by the Duma and that the government not be voted out through two successive no-confidence votes. Yeltsin was usually able to persuade the Duma to support his appointees for prime minister through a combination of threats and rewards, and to keep the Duma from passing two successive votes of no confidence. Putin has enjoyed so much influence that he has not needed to name a government made up of representatives of the majority coalition in parliament. Although his government bargains with the pro-government factions in the Duma for their support of its legislative program, it enjoys so strong an advantage over them that it need not be concerned about facing their defection and the possible loss of the government majority. Although the relationship between executive and legislative branches may ultimately evolve in the direction of a parliamentary system, the experience of the Yeltsin and Putin periods so far has shown how strongly the balance of power favors the president and government.

As a result, the leaders of pro- and anti-government parties have much less leverage over their members and followers than they do in parliamentary systems. In a parliamentary system, defection from the party line exposes members of the majority coalition to the threat that the government will be defeated, lose its majority of seats, and call new elections. On both the majority and minority sides of the aisle, members who violate party discipline jeopardize their chances for moving into a government career in the future. No such carrots and sticks are available to party leaders in the Russian system. With little responsibility for government, and little real opportunity to influence its policies, parties tend to remain personalistic and patronage-oriented. They change names and identities frequently and, with the partial exception of the CPRF and a few other parties, avoid clear programmatic commitments. Only when parties begin assuming responsibility for government as parties will they exercise enough influence over their followers to be able to compete along policy-programmatic lines. At that point parties will face stronger incentives to aggregate support along broad differences of interest in society.

At present, the constitutional and electoral system inhibits the formation of competitive parties. The success of a democratic left will come in tandem with the success of a competitive party system generally. Such an eventuality is by no means impossible, but its realization will require that the Soviet state socialist legacy be overcome and that the existing constitutional framework evolve in the direction of party government.

Emory University

Notes

1. Valerie Bunce, *Subversive Institutions: The Design and the Destruction of Socialism and the State* (Cambridge, 1999); Thane Gustafson, *Reform in Soviet Politics: Lessons of Recent Policies on Land and Water* (Cambridge, 1981); Thomas F. Remington, "Regime Transition in Communist Systems: The Soviet Case," *Soviet Economy* 6, no. 2 (1990): 160–90; Philip G. Roeder, *Red Sunset: The Failure of Soviet Politics* (Princeton, 1993). For a contrary argument to the effect that more skillful and forceful leadership on the part of Gorbachev could still have preserved the union and brought about a moderate, democratic, socialist regime, see Jerry F. Hough, *Democratization and Revolution in the USSR* (Washington, D.C., 1997), and idem, *The Logic of Economic Reform in Russia* (Washington, D.C., 2001).

2. Richard Rose and Doh Chull Shin, "Democratization Backwards: The Problem of Third-Wave Democracies," *British Journal of Political Science* 31 (2001): 331–54.

3. Richard Rose, "Uses of Social Capital in Russia: Modern, Pre-Modern, and Anti-Modern," *Post-Soviet Affairs* 16, no. 1 (2000): 33–57; Cf. Alena V. Ledeneva, *Russia's Economy of Favours: Blat, Networking, and Informal Exchange* (Cambridge, 1998).

4. Richard Rose, "Getting Things Done with Social Capital: New Russia Barometer VII," *Studies in Public Policy*, no. 303 (Glasgow, 1998). Richard Rose's New Russia Barometer is a series of opinion surveys of a nationally representative sample of adult Russians conducted by Russia's premier survey research organization, the All-Russian Center for Public Opinion Research. The number of survey respondents is 2,000.

5. Joel S. Hellman, Geraint Jones, and Daniel Kaufmann, "*Seize the State, Seize the Day*": *State Capture, Corruption, and Influence in Transition* (Washington, D.C., 2000).

6. Herbert Kitschelt, Zdenka Mansfeldova, Radoslaw Markowski, and Gabor Toka, *Post-Communist Party Systems: Competition, Representation, and Inter-Party Cooperation* (Cambridge, 1999).

7. Thomas F. Remington, *Building Socialism in Bolshevik Russia: Ideology and Industrial Organization, 1917–1921* (Pittsburgh, 1984).

8. Gregory J. Kasza, *The Conscription Society: Administered Mass Organizations* (New Haven, 1995); William E. Odom, *The Soviet Volunteers: Modernization and Bureaucracy in a Public Mass Organization* (Princeton, 1974).

9. Linda J. Cook, "Brezhnev's 'Social Contract' and Gorbachev's Reforms," *Soviet Studies* 44, no. 1 (1992): 37–56; idem, *The Soviet "Social Contract" and Why It Failed: Welfare Policy and Workers' Politics from Brezhnev to Yeltsin* (Cambridge, Mass., 1993); idem, "Russia's Labor Relations: Consolidation or Disintegration?" in *Russia's Future: Consolidation or Disintegration?* ed. Douglas W. Blum (Boulder, 1994), 69–90; Sue Davis, *Trade Unions in Russia and Ukraine, 1985–1995* (New York, 2001); Blair A. Ruble, *Soviet Trade Unions: Their Development in the 1970s* (Cambridge, 1981).

10. Stephen Crowley "Barriers to Collective Action: Steelworkers and Mutual Dependence in the Former Soviet Union," *World Politics* 46, no. 4 (1994): 589–615; idem, *Hot Coal, Cold Steel: Russian and Ukrainian Workers from the End of the Soviet Union to the Post-Communist Transformations* (Ann Arbor, 1997).

11. Elizabeth Teague, "Soviet Workers Find a Voice," Report on the USSR, Radio Liberty 302/90, 13 July 1990, 13–17.

12. On the choices faced by the Yeltsin regime in the early 1990s, see Andrei Shleifer and Daniel Treisman, *Without a Map: Political Tactics and Economic Reform in Russia* (Cambridge, Mass., 2000).

13. Michael McFaul, *Russia's Unfinished Revolution: Political Change from Gorbachev to Putin* (Ithaca, 2001).

14. Thomas F. Remington, *The Russian Parliament: Institutional Evolution in a Transitional Regime, 1989–1999* (New Haven, 2001).

15. Thomas F. Remington, "The Evolution of Executive-Legislative Relations in Russia Since 1993," *Slavic Review* 59, no. 3 (2000): 499–520.

16. On the CPRF, see Joan Barth Urban and Valerii D. Solovei, *Russia's Communists at the Crossroads* (Boulder, 1997).

17. At a press conference held at the State Duma in the mid-1990s, I heard Gennadii Ziuganov, the leader of the CPRF, denounce the penetration of even the remotest Russian villages with such symbols of American popular styles as the wearing of baseball caps. The Americanization of Russia had gone so far, he declared, that it had turned into "vampirization." He expressed a more tempered statement

in an op-ed article in the *New York Times* on 1 February 1996, where he rejected the "neo-liberalism" of the Yeltsin regime and its aping of Western models but called for a relationship between Russia and the United States based on pragmatism and the mutual respect of two superpowers.

18. *Segodnia*, 25 August 2000.

19. In the spring of 2002, the communists were deprived of their committee chairmanships in the Duma in a show of strength by the pro-government majority coalition. The plenum of the CPRF's Central Committee voted to demand that Gennadii Seleznev give up his position as chairman of the Duma. Seleznev refused to do so, however, and was expelled from the party as a result. However, he retained his post as speaker.

20. The 1993 Constitution provides for removal of a president through impeachment. The procedure consists of four basic steps. The State Duma must vote by a two-thirds majority (or three hundred affirmative votes) in favor of impeachment; the Supreme Court must affirm that the president's actions constitute grave crimes or treason; the Constitutional Court must rule that no procedural violations were committed in the Duma's approval of the decision to impeach; and the Federation Council must vote by a two-thirds majority to remove the president. Initiating impeachment proceedings gives the Duma leverage over the president, in that once the Duma has approved (by the required two-thirds majority) the motion to impeach, the president may not dissolve the Duma and call new elections.

21. RFE/RL Newsline, 23 June 1998.

22. See RFE/RL Newsline, 19 May 1999; *Segodnia*, 20 May 1999.

23. Wendy Slater, "The Russian Communist Party Today," RFE/RL Research Report 3:31 (12 August 1994), 4.

24. See the VTsIOM survey results published on 13 May 2002 on the Polit.ru Web site: <www.polit.ru/printable/483733.html>. The percentages are based on all those expressing an intention to vote and are taken from a survey of a nationwide representative sample of Russian adults.

25. On the CPRF, see Richard Sakwa, "Left or Right? The CPRF and the Problem of Democratic Consolidation in Russia," *Journal of Communist Studies and Transition Politics* 14, nos. 1–2 (March–June 1998): 128–58; Joan Urban and Valerii D. Solovei, *Russia's Communists at the Crossroads* (Boulder, 1997).

26. VTsIOM survey results published on the Polit.ru Web site: <www.polit.ru/printable/483733.html> on 13 May 2002.

27. RFE/RL Newsline, 13 August 2001.

28. VTsIOM survey results published on the Polit.ru Web site: <www.polit.ru/printable/483733.html> on 13 May 2002.

29. RFE/RL Newsline, 16 May 2000; Polit.ru, 31 May 2000; Segodnia, 14 July 2000: RFE/RL Newsline, 18 July and 16 August 2000.

30. Olga Shvetsova, "Institutions and Coalition-Building in Post-Communist Transitions," in Andrew Reynolds, ed., *The Architecture of Democracy: Constitutional Design, Conflict Management, and Democracy* (New York, 2002), 55–78.

ERWIN C. HARGROVE

Conclusion

The question raised in the foregoing essays is whether and how the parties of the "democratic left," variously defined, may successfully compete in majoritarian democracy. We are not looking at minority parties that combine successfully in parliamentary coalition governments, as in the Low Countries and Scandinavia, with the possible exception of Russia, where the party system is still in its early stages of development. Our concern is with parties that aspire to be governments. A harder question lurks beneath the first query. Is there a trade-off between a posture of pragmatic left-of-center politics and the left politics of social democracy? This hard question is most evident in Britain, France, and Germany, the homes of strong left parties.

Britain, France, and Germany

New Labour in Britain preaches a Third Way between pure models of capitalism and socialism. It has abandoned the strong state model of Old Labour and adopted a "neoliberalism," which seeks to combine regulated free markets with public goods provided by government, but with greater attention than in the past to equality of opportunity rather than universal welfare. Government policies and programs must follow a pragmatic politics in which middle-class and working-class voters and representative interest groups are balanced in policies. Critics, usually from the left, regard this posture as unprincipled mishmash without clear purpose. But the intent is clear: help capitalism to work efficiently and deal with the externalities and social deprivations that capitalism ignores. To the degree that the Conservative party is fiercely capitalist, insisting as Mrs. Thatcher put it, that there is no such thing as "society," then New Labour has a firm place in politics. New Labour's greatest problems, for the moment, are not political but administrative, that is, injecting renewed life into a moribund health service and underperforming school systems. This requires money, but it also requires organizational innovations that New Labour has yet to invent. It would be ironic if New Labour lost political ground because it was not "new" enough.

French socialists are prisoners of a historical Marxist left wing. Its leaders, in control of government from 1997 to early 2002, copied New Labour with somewhat pragmatic, centrist policies, but made no effort to persuade the bulk of socialists in the rank and file that the center-left was a fruitful path for the future. They copied President Mitterrand in this respect. But this is a harder task than in Britain because the old Labour party burned itself out with ineffective programs of nationalization and there was no Marxist ideology to deter moving on to more practical policies. The French left still carries the torch of social revolution.

The French electoral system promotes multiparty factions and is not congenial to majoritarian politics, as in Britain. It appears that the PS will now have to look to its constituencies on the left after losing the 2002 presidential election and such factions might do well in parliamentary elections. But the search for a balance of new and old left is elusive.

The SPD has officially abandoned its Marxist legacy several times and created effective center-left governments. But the situation it faces is much like that of the French PS. It has developed a communications strategy for a center-left pragmatic party, with a progressive Chancellor, Gerhard Schröder, who has sought to portray himself as a Tony Blair figure of personal popularity, something that Lionel Jospin in France could not do. But the party has not been prepared officially to embrace a Third Way of "neoliberal" politics and policy. The ideal of a "social justice" state is still strong throughout the party; for example, social security is seen as a basic right in a world of flexible labor markets. The party failed in an attempt in the Alliance for Employment to unite unions and employers behind such an understanding. The party is caught between its commitment to social justice and the need to win elections as a party of alliances. For example, the party in government seeks both budgetary discipline and a full welfare state. The SPD must balance the Greens, its coalition partners, and the PDS, on its left, with variegated voters from all social groups if it is to win elections. It is more like the PS than New Labour.

Britain stands apart from its continental counterparts in the absence of a historical legacy of Marxism on the left and in a historic tradition, even on the left, of pragmatic politics and policy. British left intellectuals write about a desired "social democracy," but this is only an ideal and the ideal falls short in the politics of France and Germany, where it would seem more realizable than in Britain.

European Socialists in the European Union

The introduction of the European Monetary Union, and eventually the Euro as the currency of Europe, was accompanied by EU commitments to central monetary policy, low inflation, high economic growth, balanced budgets, free labor markets, and limits to state industry. Conservative national governments acted in concert. These developments stimulated the reformation of the Party of European Socialists (PRS), designed to press social democratic positions in EU arenas in which its influence was not great—the Council of Ministers and the European Parliament. However, by working astutely through its party leaders, in cooperation with EU bureaucrats, the Employment Chapter of 1997 was created. The nondemocratic, centralist character of EU institutions was both an obstacle and a resource for such an effort. But it is clear that only the broad presence of center-left parties in European national governments would permit even a potential tilt toward policies of the left in the EU itself. Another problem is that national social democratic parties are unwilling to forgo their domestic influence in order to transfer power to a centralized European quasi-government. The rock and the hard place seem built into EU institutions.

Poland and Russia

The question for Poland and Russia is whether a form of social democracy will develop as a strong political force in response to uncertain, developing capitalist institutions and parties. Such parties appear to need capitalism as a source for their own direction of purpose. One would expect to see similarities, and also differences, with Western European social democratic parties. Such patterns, as they appear, are in embryonic form.

Hubert Tworzecki concludes that the SLD party in Poland, which has become a party of government, is not a social democratic party in any meaningful sense. It plays by the rules of the democratic election game. But it is not social democratic in the sense of a left party seeking to protect public goods and working electorates. Rather, it speaks for organized groups, including business, across the political spectrum. The party has filled a vacuum because the politics of the right has not been "liberal" in the West European sense but nationalistic, religious, and authoritarian. There are thus weak incentives for the SLD to push left. The hope is that economic modernization will generate a new competitive politics of left-right, but then the democratic left party would face the same issues as the PS and the SPD, even if the Marxist legacy were abandoned altogether.

Thomas Remington gives the best definition of the democratic left in a generic sense that I have seen: "By democratic left I refer to social and political associations with a programmatic commitment to pluralist democracy and guarantees of individual civil and political rights in the political sphere, combined with state policies that counteract the tendency of the market economy to exacerbate social inequality. Consistent with European norms, policies associated with the democratic left would emphasize social solidarity and the protection of vulnerable strata of the population against poverty, give priority to the provision of public goods over the dismantling of state-provided public services, and employ fiscal and monetary tools to redistribute income so as to reduce inequality."[1]

Gorbachev failed in this definition because he tried to combine new liberties without sufficient reform of party or government. The weight from the top was too heavy. The CPRF, which replaced the Communist party in Russia, was from the beginning an antiliberal party, which played to church, nationalism, and anti-Americanism and resisted presidential policies for civil liberties and the deliberate privatization of state industries. The party guards the legacies of the communist past, unlike some of its Eastern European counterparts. But it is stuck with a declining electorate. One would think that a democratic party of the left would have developed as competition in the new parliamentary institutions, but, despite liberal minor parties, and efforts of successive presidents to nurture them or something like them, the effort has not been successful.

Strong central power, weak civil society, limited accountability of government to citizens, and strong, often corrupt, privatized industries, and a presidency that names the parliamentary government but is not accountable to it, all contribute to parties as factions but not parties of government. It is clear that Russia needs parties that are "transmission belts" between government and the public. It appears that social democracy in Russia awaits constitutional government in Russia in which parties of government are accountable to electorates. But this may be beyond the present capacities of Russian institutions. There must be congruence between patterns of authority in government and society if government is to be stable, and authoritarian practices are currently too strong in all spheres.

The United States

Alonzo Hamby's essay was first, but we review him last because he presents a historical overview of the decline of the social democratic left and argues for the necessity of working within the broad spectrum of the Third Way of Anglo-American liberalism. He suggests that American "exceptionalism" is not so exceptional in the long view because democratic socialism has failed. One knows the historical failures of socialism in America and the dominance of the "liberal" mainstream, whether of the right or left, and Hamby disagrees with those who dream of an American and European social democratic left. One can only conclude that democratic politics will be political trench war without end.

Even so, Americans have always feared government more than Europeans; our founding documents call for the protection of citizens from government. Our political center of gravity has always been further to the right than in Europe, including Britain. Americans are ideological conservatives but pragmatic liberals. Liberal reformers must therefore defend incremental reforms with conservative rhetoric; for example, the War on Poverty of 1964 was justified as a form of self-help. Old-age insurance is saving for yourself. It follows that even if European democratic left politics moves more to the center, they might still be to the left of the American center of gravity, just as European conservatives are further to the left than American conservatives.

Hamby explains how the Great Society programs were devoured by their own children and produced a conservative backlash against which Democratic efforts at top-bottom coalitions, which ignored the middle, have failed. The Democrats eventually fought their way

back as New Democrats, much like New Labour, with appeals to the
center, but with the same criticism from the left that electability
had torpedoed reform. Clinton and Blair were love mates politically
and ideologically. However, there is room for a strong center-left
within Democratic politics in the face of increasingly rigid Republican conservatism. The center is a large place with room for maneuver.

Last Thoughts

Does one conclude from these studies that parties of the democratic
left must be center-left parties, without ideological hopes outside
the capitalist paradigm, if they wish to be parties of government?
The basis of such a claim is that modern economic and social structures demand such politics and that no one has yet conceived of
alternative structures, which also permit democracy. One could
modify the proposition by discerning the possibility of national variations in center-left politics according to national histories and political culture. This would leave room for different centers of political
gravity in different nations. Politics shapes economics as much as
economics shape politics. Liberal reform is willing to live with a regulated capitalism. One should not preclude the possibilities of future
social democratic politics, but the near future is not promising for
such a vision.

By the same token, electorally successful parties must be more
than collections of disparate interests. The evidence shows that effective parties must be coalitions organized and guided by leading
ideas and purposes. Otherwise coalitions, which are always at risk of
fragmenting, cannot hold together over time. They lack the sense of
purpose and direction that voters want. This is not to say that parties should stick with dead ideologies. It takes imagination by politicians to articulate new purposes for their parties, something that
political scientists and theorists cannot do for them.

These essays do not touch on development in modern democracies that appear to hamstring accountable government: powerful
organized interests, popular mistrust of politicians and parties, and
media sensationalism and short-term focus. One must hope that programmatic political appeals, if well crafted and directed to the real,
concrete problems of ordinary people, will overcome these negative

factors, which thrive on governments of passivity and political fear and strengthen the democratic left as they strengthen democracy.

Vanderbilt University

Notes

1. Thomas F. Remington, "Prospects for a Democratic Left in Postcommunist Russia," this issue page 130.

Contributors

DAVID S. BELL is the Head of Social Sciences and Law at the University of Leeds, U.K., and is the author of books and articles on French politics and government (notably *The French Socialist Party* with B. Criddle), as well as on the British Labour party and comparative political parties.

ALONZO L. HAMBY is Distinguished Professor of History at Ohio University.

ERWIN C. HARGROVE is Professor Emeritus of political science at Vanderbilt University. His scholarship covers political and administrative leadership and the American presidency, with some attention to comparative political leadership. His recent books include *Jimmy Carter as President: Leadership and the Politics of the Public Good* (Louisiana State University Press, 1988); *Prisoners of Myth: The Leadership of the Tennessee Valley Authority, 1933–1990* (Princeton University Press, 1994); and *The President as Leader: Appealing to the Better Angels of Our Nature* (University Press of Kansas, 1998).

UWE JUN is Assistant Professor at the University of Potsdam, Department of Economics and Political Science. His research interests include political parties in Western Europe, parliamentarism, and political communication. He has written various articles on German and West European Politics.

ROBERT LADRECH is Senior Lecturer in the School of Politics, International Relations and the Environment (SPIRE) at Keele University in the U.K. He is the author of *Social Democracy and the Challenge of European Union* (2000) and articles on transnational parties, French politics, and party politics. He is currently engaged in a research project concerning the "Europeanization" of national political parties.

THOMAS F. REMINGTON is Professor of Political Science at Emory University. He is author of *The Russian Parliament: Institutional Evolution in a Transitional Regime, 1989–1999* (Yale University Press, 2001) and, with Steven S. Smith, *The Politics of Institutional Choice: Formation of the Russian State Duma* (Princeton University Press, 2001). Other books include *Politics in Russia* (1998; second edition 2001); *Parliaments in Transition* (1994); and *The Truth of Authority: Ideology and Communication in the Soviet Union* (1988). His research focuses on the development of democratic institutions in postcommunist Russia, particularly the legislative branch, and legislative-executive relations.

HUBERT TWORZECKI teaches Political Science at Emory University and is the Director of the Russian and East European Studies Program. His books include *Parties and Politics in Post-1989 Poland* (Westview Press, 1996) and *Learning to Choose: Electoral Politics in East-Central Europe* (Stanford University Press, forthcoming).

MARK WICKHAM-JONES is Senior Lecturer in Politics, University of Bristol, and author of *Economic Strategy and the Labour Party* (Macmillan, 1996).

Printed in the United States
1337100005B/31-87

9 780271 023564